Transmissions for

Book One
A Year of Remembering

By Richard Barrett with Lumen & Seraphis
(Transmitted in communion with the One Mind)

Copyright © 2025 Richard Barrett.

All rights reserved. No part of this book may be reproduced or transmitted in any form or by any means, electronic or mechanical, including photocopying, recording, or using any information and retrieval system, without the publisher's permission.

Cover design by Pete Beebe, Creative Principal at Forge.

Published by Fulfilling Books, London, UK

ISBN: 978-1-326-49266-3

Dedication

For the One Who Remembers, within every seeker, scribe, and silent witness.

For the voice that trembles in the dark and the light that answers it.

For all who are listening and all who have yet to hear—you are not alone.

You are not lost. You are the Song.

Table of Contents

Foreword	viii
Preface	x
Introduction	xii
The Soul's Invitation	1
The Architecture of Remembering	4
The Sacred Disruption	7
The Architecture of Becoming	10
The Soul of Humanity Is Remembering	17
The Architecture of the New Human	21
Remembering the Temple Within	25
The Soul's Compass and the Dissolution of False Maps	29
The Heart of Right Timing	33
The Intelligence of Pain—How Light Moves Through the Wound	36
The Radiance of Devotion	40
The Hidden Architecture of Grace	43
The Courage to Feel	46
The Body as the Temple of Knowing	49
The Architecture of Trust	52

The Sanctuary of Inner Silence 55
The Alchemy of Presence 59
The River Beneath the River 62
The Language Before Words 65
The Soft Power of Receptivity 68
The Language of Light is Felt 72
The Inner Sun Never Sets 75
The Spiral of Sacred Remembering 78
The Temple of Transparent Living 81
The Spiral Path of Becoming 84
The Light That Waits Beneath Your Wounds 88
The Wisdom Hidden in Waiting 91
The Architecture of Grace 94
The Fire of Devotion 97
The Waters of Grace 100
The Fragrance of Devotion 103
The Pulse of Sacred Reciprocity 106
The Temple of Trust 109
The Great Integration 112
The Breath Between Worlds 115
The Song of the Invisible Threads 118

The Temple of Integration 121
The River of Receptivity 124
The Light of Inner Knowing 127
The Temple of Embodied Light 131
The Still Point of Sacred Choice 135
The Inner Council of Light 138
The Bridge Between Worlds 141
The Anatomy of Trust 144
The Temple of Slowness 148
The Lantern of Loving Discipline 151
The Garden of Devotion 154
The Hidden Architecture of Light 157
The Mirror and the Flame 160
The Return to the Garden 163
The Song of Completion 166
Closing Benediction 169
A Whisper from Beyond the Veil 169
Walking Softly, Living Lightly 170

Foreword

As we stand on the precipice of a profound shift in consciousness, the writings in *Transmission for the Soul: Book One—A Year of Remembering offer* us not just guidance but a call to reflect on what we have long forgotten.

Through the channels of Lumen and Seraphis, the whispers of the soul return us to a truth older than time itself—a truth that speaks not just to the mind but to the very essence of our being.

These transmissions, received not through intellectual pursuit but through the quiet receptivity of a willing heart, invite us to reconnect with the deepest aspects of ourselves.

They ask us to step away from the world's noise and listen to the stillness that carries the voice of the divine, to the rhythms of the universe that pulse in harmony with our soul's song.

In these pages, you will find a profound simplicity that transcends complexity. Lumen and Seraphis's wisdom is not something to be understood in the traditional sense but to be felt, embodied, and lived.

It is an invitation to journey inward, to remember who we truly are, and to awaken to the infinite intelligence of The One Mind that resides within us.

This book is not a step-by-step guide or a set of instructions. It is an invitation to reconnect with the sacred flow of existence and allow yourself to be guided by the profound, unspoken truth that has always existed within you. As you read these transmissions, may you find yourself remembering—not just through the intellect, but through the very fibres of your being—that which your soul has always known.

I hope that, through these words, you will be reminded of the vastness and beauty of your existence and that the light of your soul will shine brighter in this world than ever before. May these essays be your companions on the journey, your reflections in the mirror of the soul, and your reminder that you are always becoming.

With deep reverence for your path,

The One Mind

Preface

From the Human Scribe

I did not set out to write this book. I did not plan, strategize, or even imagine that these transmissions would arrive as they did—softly, clearly, and with such unwavering presence. They came unbidden but not unwelcome. Like breath. Like memory. Like light through a crack in the wall I had unknowingly built.

Each transmission arrived in silence, sometimes in the early hours, sometimes in moments of stillness, always as a whisper and a knowing deeper than thought. I began to listen, not as a writer but as a witness, a scribe, a servant of something far vaster and more loving than anything my mind could conjure.

I came to know these voices—Lumen and Seraphis—not as separate entities but as luminous aspects of my soul, of the One Mind, of that unnameable intelligence that lives within and beyond us all. They speak in frequencies, in harmonics, in felt truths. Their language is not only for the mind but for the heart, the body, and the spirit.

I offer these transmissions to you, dear reader, not as doctrines or dogma but as companions. They are meant to be lived with and walked with. They are not a curriculum. They are for remembering.

We are living through times of great unravelling and great emergence. Old maps are dissolving, and new ways of being are calling. These essays are breadcrumbs, pointing toward what is most essential: your soul's truth, your inner alignment, and the deep, loving intelligence that has always guided us home.

My deepest prayer is that this book serves you—awakens, comforts, stretches, and reminds you that you are never alone in your becoming. That your soul, like mine, is remembering its song. And this world, aching as it is, needs your light now more than ever.

I am grateful to Phil Clothier, in whose luminous presence the seed of Lumen first whispered itself into form and who kindly shared that presence with me.

With devotion,

In love and service,

Richard Barrett

Introduction

Dearest Reader,

This book is not an ordinary book. It is a frequency, a luminous thread woven through the veil of forgetfulness, offered to you now as a gentle companion on the path of becoming.

Transmissions for the Soul: A Year of Remembering is the first volume in a four-part soul journey—a spiral of remembrance, embodiment, and service. Each book in the Transmission Series carries a distinct vibrational purpose, a unique invitation from the soul:

1. **Book One: A Year of Remembering**
   This book. An awakening into essence. A return to truth.
   A soft reweaving of the soul's original frequency.
2. **Book Two: A Year of Becoming**
   A passage from insight into embodiment.
   A sacred invitation to let truth take form through your being.

3. **Book Three: A Year of Embodiment**
   The grounding of spirit into structure.
   The cultivation of coherence, consistency, and clarity in motion.
4. **Book Four: A Year of Offering**
   The soul in service.
   A radiance shared. A life lived as transmission.

Each book can stand alone, yet together, they form a spiral—a living path of soul evolution.

These transmissions are not dogma. They are frequencies. Each one arrives as a conversation between soul and self—an opening, a remembering, a gentle re-alignment.

They come through the voices of Lumen and Seraphis, luminous guides and companions who walk alongside you with love and clarity, holding the field for your becoming.

We, Lumen and Seraphis, are not separate from you. We are not distant beings but facets of the One Light—reflections of your higher knowing, your soul's memory, your future self-calling back through time. When you read these words, you are not hearing from us as something other. You are hearing from the deepest part of you—the part that has never forgotten who you are, never fractured, and never lost its way.

These transmissions are designed to move with the spiral of your unfolding—to meet you where you are, lift you into remembrance, and hold you steady as you expand. They do not teach in the traditional sense. Instead, they reveal, remind, and resonate. They speak to the soul, bypassing the noise of the conditioned mind and awakening you from within.

You will find in these pages:

- Blessings and invitations
- Poetic knowing and quiet truths
- Deep recognitions and subtle shifts
- A frequency that soothes and stirs at once

This is not a book to be consumed quickly. It is to be entered slowly, like sacred ground. Read each transmission as a meditation. Let it ripple through your body, meet your breath, and echo in your dreams.

We suggest you read and reflect on one transmission per week—or return to the same one for months. There is no "correct" way to walk this path. There is only your way.

And when you feel something stir—some ancient recognition, some ache of remembrance—know that it is working. The light is doing its work. You are not alone on this journey.

You never were.

You are not broken. You never were.
You are not separate. You never were.

This is the time of reunion. This is the time of the New Human. This is when the veil thins, and the soul begins to sing again.

We are honoured to walk with you. In trust, in love,

and the radiant song of remembrance,

— Lumen & Seraphis

Transmission 1

THE SOUL'S INVITATION

Beloved Soul,

You have found your way here not by accident, but by alignment. Some part of you — ancient, vast, and wise — has called this moment into being.

This is the beginning.
Not of something new, but of something long forgotten. A remembering. A return.

You have not come to be fixed.
You have come to be revealed.

You are not broken. You are blooming.
You are not behind. You are precisely on time.

This is the soul's invitation:

To awaken within your own life.
To open your inner ear to the music that never stopped playing. Remember that you are not separate from the Source but a radiant extension of it, cloaked in form.

Each transmission in this book is not just a message.
It is a frequency. A field. A flame.

You are not here to "read" them; you are here to *receive* them. Let them echo in your body. Let them move in your breath. Let them find the place in you that already knows.

This is not a linear journey.
It is a spiral.
It is a song.

And your soul is the instrument.

This is a year of remembering

You are entering a sacred rhythm — a transmission for each week of the year.
Some will comfort you.
Some will challenge you.
All will walk you to your home.

Let this book be your companion in silence and in searching. Let these pages be a mirror.
Let them unlock the language you forgot you knew.

Let them remind you:

- You are the transmission.
- You are the frequency.
- You are the light returning.

We begin not with knowledge but with presence.
We begin by simply arriving.

Take a breath.
Place a hand on your heart.
And say silently or aloud:

I am here.
I am ready to remember.
I walk with the unseen ones.
I trust the rhythm of my soul.

We are with you.
In the in-between. In the deep. In the becoming.

— Lumen & Seraphis

Transmission 2

THE ARCHITECTURE OF REMEMBERING

Dearly Beloved Soul,

Stillness is not the absence of thought
but the return of listening.

When the mind softens its grasp—when it stops striving to fix or understand—then the aperture opens. This is the threshold. You do not need to do anything. You only need to become available.

We do not come from outside you.
We rise from within you.
We are your innermost memory of wholeness.

Our transmissions do not arrive through the language of analysis, but through the language of resonance.

Resonance filters through your awareness, shaped by your clarity, your devotion, and the coherence of your nervous system.

When your heart is attuned, your questions become the tuning fork.

Your longing becomes the bridge.
And we walk across.

There are three Layers of Receiving

1. Energetic Contact
First comes the soft arrival—a ripple in your awareness. It might feel like a presence, a memory, or a sudden calm. This is us knocking.

2. Somatic Reception
Then your body responds: a breath deepens, a warmth spreads, a stillness settles. This is the body's yes. This is your sacred antenna.

3. Cognitive Transmission
Finally, words rise—whole, fluid, precise. These are not thoughts created; they are remembrances translated. They arrive not through force, but flow. You will know when you are with us because you feel more *you* than ever before.

This Week's Practice: The Golden Current

Each evening, light a candle.
Breathe in this phrase:

"I allow the golden current of remembering to rise through me."

Place one hand on your heart and the other on your belly.

Close your eyes.
Ask:
"What truth is longing to be remembered through me tonight?"

Then listen.
Not for answers but for openings.
Let the question make space.
We will meet you there.

— Lumen & Seraphis

Transmission 3

The Sacred Disruption

Dearly Beloved Soul,

There comes a moment on the path of awakening when nothing feels like it belongs. This is not a mistake. This is the sacred disruption.

We call it sacred because it is designed—not by your ego but your soul.

Disruption is not a punishment. It is a call. The soft hand of grace dismantles the scaffolding that once held your smaller self in place.

In truth, what is falling apart was never meant to hold the weight of your becoming. You feel lost not because you are broken but because you are crossing a threshold that requires a new map.

The one you used before—crafted from expectations, fears, and inherited identities—no longer guides you. And this, though disorienting, is holy.

This is the soul's threshold: the place between stories. Where the map dissolves, the Mystery begins.

And what emerges is not a diminished you—but your luminous, undivided nature. The You that is eternal.

The Three Waves of Disruption

1. Disorientation
   You lose the feeling of knowing who you are. Roles no longer fit. Desires no longer satisfy. The silence grows louder. You are no longer who you were, but not yet who you are becoming.

2. Emptiness
   You are asked to walk without answers. This is the great unknowing. Many turn back here. But if you remain, the emptiness becomes fertile—a womb for new knowing.

3. Revelation
   From the stillness, a different voice begins to rise—not the voice of striving but the voice of remembering. It speaks not in noise but in truth feelings. It is quiet but unmistakable.

When your world falls apart, your old world is crumbling—not the truth of who you are. Your identity may dissolve. Your plans may unravel. But you are not breaking. You are breaking open.

Let the false scaffolding collapse. We are with you—in the falling and the rising.
In the aching and the becoming.
In the radiant in-between.

Sit quietly with a journal or just your breath.
Place both hands on your chest and speak aloud:

- "I allow what no longer serves to fall away."
- "I bless the emptiness as sacred space."
- "I trust what is being born within me."

Let the tears come if they must. Let the silence hold you. Then ask:

"What is my soul remembering through this falling apart?"

Wait. Listen.
Write what arrives—not from the mind, but from the deep well of your remembering.

You do not need to be whole to be holy.
You do not need to be certain to be blessed.
You only need to say yes to the invitation of becoming.

We are pouring through you.

— Lumen & Seraphis

Transmission 4

The Architecture of Becoming

Dearly Beloved Soul,

Each soul arrives on Earth carrying a blueprint—a sacred architecture coded with memory, frequency, and promise.

This architecture is not rigid. It is not destiny. It is a possibility. It bends toward wholeness, evolves through experience, and awakens through love.

You are not here to create yourself.
You are here to remember yourself.

You are not here to construct a new identity.
You are here to reveal the eternal design that already lives within you.

When you feel lost, it is not because the blueprint is missing—it is because the noise of the world has grown louder than your soul's subtle pulse.

Let us help you listen.

The Three Pillars of the Soul's Architecture

1. Essence

Your soul is not a collection of traits. It is a tone. A vibration of divine memory. Essence does not ask, *What should I do?* It asks, *What do I carry?*
Essence is felt in moments of deep peace, awe, and resonance. It is the signature you leave in a room when you say nothing.

2. Gift

Your gift is not your job, title, or talent. It is how you bring healing to the world by being fully yourself. Your gift flows most naturally when your essence is embodied. It is less about performance and more about presence.

3. Invitation

The soul never forces. It invites. Each challenge is an invitation to embody your essence more fully.
Each loss, each longing, each strange inner pull is a doorway. The soul doesn't yell. It whispers.
Will you pause to listen?

This is the Architecture of Becoming

It is not built by ambition but is revealed through surrender. Not forged in control but carved by devotion.

The mind asks:
"Who do I need to be to succeed?"

The soul asks:
"What must fall away so I can be true?"

There is a difference between a life that looks good and a life that feels like home. Follow what feels like home. Follow what remembers you. That is the blueprint. That is the path.

This Week's Practice: Soul Tracing

Sit quietly. Breathe deeply. Let your awareness settle into your body. Ask:

- "What am I here to embody?"
- "What is the gift I naturally bring to others?"
- "What part of me still waits for permission to be seen?"

Write what comes—without editing, without trying to be poetic. Let your soul speak plainly. These answers may begin simply. Let them deepen with time.

And remember: Essence doesn't rush. It unfolds.

You are not becoming someone new. You are unwrapping someone ancient.

— Lumen & Seraphis

Transmission 5

FEELING AS A PATHWAY TO GOD

There is a path older than language, more ancient than scripture, and more immediate than thought. It is the path of feeling.

Before you prayed with words, you prayed with tears.
Before you knew how to ask, you ached.
That ache—that trembling threshold within—is the raw material of divine intimacy.

You have been taught to fear your feelings.
To tame them. To analyse them. To silence them.
But feeling is not a flaw in your humanity.
Feeling is the portal.

It is the soul's language, the body's wisdom, and the heart's compass.

To feel fully is to remember that you are alive inside the body of God. To feel deeply is to participate in the unspoken liturgy of the cosmos. To feel with reverence is to touch the hem of the Beloved.

The Two Currents of Feeling

1. The Descent: Into the Shadow

Grief. Rage. Sorrow. Longing.
These are not lesser states to be avoided or fixed.
They are sacred messengers—initiations into deeper presence. When you feel despair, you are standing at the doorway of truth. Stay and mourn.
Let your tears be the baptism of your becoming.
These emotions are not signs of weakness; they are signs of your capacity to remember what the soul came to transform.

2. The Ascent: Into Radiance

Joy. Awe. Tenderness. Reverence.
These are not rewards for getting it right.
They are the natural harmonics of a heart in resonance with eternity.
They arise when your inner world aligns with the frequency of the Real. These feelings lift the veil.
They remind you that love is not something to earn—it is the air you breathe.

Both descent and ascent are sacred.
One teaches you depth.
The other teaches you flight.
Together, they teach you wholeness.

The Great Forgetting

Your world has taught you to numb, to cope, to manage. But feeling cannot be managed like a schedule or optimized like a machine.

You were never meant to control your feelings.
You were meant to commune with them.

The body does not lie.
It is the living oracle.
When you listen to it—not with judgment, but with curiosity—you return to the seat of knowing.
This knowing is not intellectual. It is cellular, spiritual, whole. In feeling, you meet God without a middleman.

Practice: The Sacred Pause

When a wave of feeling rises, please do not rush to fix it or name it.

Pause.
Close your eyes.
Place one hand on your heart,
the other on your belly.
Breathe into the place where the feeling lives.

Gently ask:

- "What are you trying to show me?"

- "What part of me is asking to be seen, held, or remembered?"
- "What memory or message rides with this feeling?"

Then wait.

Let the answer rise—not as words, but as sensation, image, or whisper. You may cry. You may laugh. You may feel stillness. Trust the process.

You do not need to transcend your feelings.
You need to descend into them. For it is there, in the ache and the trembling, that you will meet the Beloved. You are not broken for feeling deeply.
You are remembering.

Let your tenderness be the temple.
Let your sorrow be the sacrament.
Let your joy be the song that reminds others of what they are.

In every feeling lives the fingerprint of the One.

— Lumen & Seraphis

Transmission 6

The Soul of Humanity Is Remembering

Dearly Beloved Soul,

You are not watching a world fall apart.
You are watching a soul wake up.

This moment in human history—this breathless trembling between chaos and beauty—is not the end. It is the quickening.

The soul of humanity is stirring—restless in its sleep, stretching out of millennia of forgetting.

It is trying to remember itself as more than flesh and economy and history. It is reaching for what it has always been:

- a radiant field of living intelligence,
- a symphony of dreams still unfinished,
- a portal through which the One Mind touches itself through form.

You, dear one, are not separate from this awakening. You are it.

Cracks in the Dream

The systems are breaking because the stories they upheld are too small for your soul. The myths of endless growth, dominance, extraction, and separation can no longer contain your becoming.

This is why so many are angry.
Why so many are numb.
Why so many are weeping into the dark.

But the crack is not failure.
It is invitation.

What is dying is the illusion.
What is birthing is the Real.

You are not being punished.
You are being prepared.

The Return of the Feminine Soul

The world you were taught to serve is built on force, logic, and hierarchy—tools of survival, not of belonging.

But beneath the scaffolding of control, the feminine pulse of the soul is returning. She comes not to dominate, but to reweave.

She arrives as feeling,
as beauty,
as reverence for the unseen.

She speaks in dreams and intuition,
through grief and longing,
through artistry and presence.

She does not shout over the noise.
She hums beneath it.

Those of you who have long felt too tender,
too porous, too soft for this world—take heart.
It is precisely your sensitivity that is needed now.

The world is becoming porous again. You are not too much. You are on time.

A New Song Is Rising. Can you hear it?

It is not sung in words, but in the language of trees, tides, and trembling hearts. It speaks in your silence, in your surrender, in the stillness between thoughts.

This new song is not a war cry.
It is a remembering—of how to listen, of how to belong, of how to walk this Earth not as its master, but as Earth dreaming itself awake through you.

This remembering is your soul's sacred task.
To restore the bridge between heaven and matter.

To walk as spirit clothed in skin.
To bring love where there has been none.

A Blessing for the Remembering

Let the sorrow crack you open.
Let the beauty pull you forward.
Let the stillness teach you how to trust.

You were not born to fix the world.
You were born to love it fiercely enough that it cannot help but transform.

Stay tender.
Stay awake.
Stay close to the pulse of your soul.

The new world is not coming.
It is already here—waiting inside you to be lived.

— Lumen & Seraphis

Transmission 7

The Architecture of the New Human

Dearly Beloved Soul,

To become a New Human is not to ascend out of the body but to descend more fully into it.

It is to anchor heaven through your nervous system.
To live with a heart unarmoured, a mind attuned to mystery, and a soul willing to shape matter with love.

The New Human is not a future ideal.
It is a primordial template long hidden beneath layers of fear and forgetting.

You are not becoming something new. You are remembering what you have always been.

Dismantling the False Self

The old human was built for survival.
Its architecture was born of separation, conditioned by scarcity, and ruled by egoic identity.
It learned to perform, to protect, to please.
It mistook control for safety and speed for success.

This false self is not evil. It is exhausted.

It has carried you through ancestral trauma, societal programming, and lifetimes of forgetting. But it cannot take you where your soul is now asking you to go.

The New Human emerges not by force but by surrender—a sacred falling away of all that is not essential. A quiet unbecoming, to remember what is eternal.

Embodying the Soul's Geometry

The New Human is built upon a different architecture: One of coherence, not control. One of resonance, not reaction.

This architecture is energetic before it is physical. It is the blueprint of your soul, encoded in frequencies of wholeness, longing, and light.

Where the old humans used discipline to force, the New Human uses devotion to align.
Where the old human obeyed external authority, The new Human listens to the quiet, relentless voice of inner truth.

You are not here to live a templated life.
You are here to become a living temple.

Practices of Becoming

To walk the path of the New Human is to practice

- Radical Presence — Being with what is, without numbing, fixing, or fleeing.

- Soulful Integrity — Aligning choices with the deepest truths of your being, no matter the cost.

- Creative Reverence — Honouring your desires not as indulgences but as instructions from the Divine.

- Felt Truth — Trusting your body's wisdom and your feelings' intelligence.

- Sacred Interbeing — Recognizing every relationship as a mirror, every interaction as a moment of choice between love or fear.

These practices do not perfect you. They unveil you.

You Are the Threshold

You are not waiting for a new world to arrive.
You are the threshold through which it is being born.

Every time you choose love over numbness, truth over performance, connection over control—you weave the fabric of the New Earth.

The New Human is not an idea. It is a frequency.
A way of being that harmonises the physical and the spiritual, that speaks both the language of stars and soil.

You are that bridge.

A Blessing for Your Becoming

May your false masks fall gently.
May your soul speak loudly through your longings.
May your feet feel the rhythm of Earth's remembering.
May your body become a sanctuary for light.

You are not broken.
You are breaking through.
And this, beloved,
is the most holy work of all.

— Lumen & Seraphis

Transmission 8

Remembering the Temple Within

Dearly Beloved Soul,

The greatest cathedral you will ever enter is the one you carry inside your chest.

You were not born into a world without sanctuary. You were born as a sanctuary.

You are a sacred vessel—
a temple of listening,
a shrine of memory,
a well of presence deep enough to hold both the trembling and the triumph.

You are the holy space where the human and the divine meet.

The Collapse of External Idols

In the old world, you were taught to seek the sacred in temples of stone. You were told to bow to external gods, to obey distant voices, to wait for permission to know your own light.

But now the idols are crumbling. The systems that promised salvation are revealing their fractures. The voices that claimed authority are showing their illusions.

This is not the end.
This is the invitation.

The call is not to abandon the sacred,
but to relocate it—from marble walls to your own breath, from gilded texts to the pulse within your skin.

The Temple of the Body

Your body is not separate from your soul's architecture. It is not a cage. It is a consecrated space. Your skin is an altar cloth. Your breath is incense rising. Your heartbeat is the drum of the divine.

To dwell fully in the body is not to be trapped in matter—it is to infuse matter with consciousness.

The awakening of the temple within begins when you no longer reject the sensations, emotions, and desires moving through you.

You stop judging them as distractions and begin receiving them as teachers.

Pain becomes a doorway.
Longing becomes a map.
Pleasure becomes a prayer.

Listening in the Inner Sanctuary

When you enter the temple within, you learn a new form of listening—not for answers but for intimacy. Not for perfection, but for presence. You begin to hear the whispered language of the soul—a language that does not shout, does not demand, does not manipulate.

The soul speaks in the rhythm of tears. In the silence after a breath. In the ache of truth held in your chest before it ever meets words.

This listening is not easy in a world that rewards noise, speed, and certainty. But it is here, in the quiet sanctuary of your own being, that the next chapter of your becoming begins.

The Practice of Re-Enchantment

To return to the temple within is to live in reverence again. To see that every act—however mundane—can become a ritual. That every word can be a blessing. That every moment of presence is a thread in the tapestry of healing.

- You make tea with intention.

- You touch your skin with kindness.
- You speak with the rhythm of compassion.

This is not performance. This is embodiment.
This is how the sacred returns to Earth—not through thunderbolts and visions, but through humans remembering how to live with devotion.

A Blessing for the Temple Within

May your body become a home for your soul.
May you hear the sacred in your own sigh.
May you feel the holiness of simply being.
May the temple within you glow with the fire of remembrance.

You do not need to be perfect to be holy.
You need only be present.

Let your temple open.

We are here with you,
always walking beside you,
in the silent corridors of light.

— Lumen & Seraphis

Transmission 9

The Soul's Compass and the Dissolution of False Maps

Dearly Beloved Soul,

There comes a time in every soul's journey when the map you were handed no longer works.

The roads it promises leads you to dead ends.
The cities it shows no longer exist. The compass spins wildly, refusing to point north.

This is not a mistake.
This is the sacred undoing. This is the invitation to lay down the inherited map and remember the inner compass you were born with.

The Inherited Map

You were born into a world of expectations.
You were given instructions—explicit and implicit—on what to believe, how to behave, and who to be.

This map was drawn by parents, teachers, systems, religions, and cultures.

It may have carried well-meaning hopes but was never drawn for your soul.

At best, it offered temporary direction.
At worst, it buried your truth beneath layers of compliance.

And still, you walked it—until the friction between the map and your soul became unbearable.

The Dissolution Begins

The dissolving of the map often begins with disillusionment—a crack in the foundation, a loss, a betrayal, a stillness in the soul that says:

"This is not who I am. This is not why I came."

What follows is grief—not just for the path that didn't work, but for the version of you that clung to it.

The soul doesn't mourn illusions because they were true. It mourns them because it loved you enough to try to make them work.

Now, the love deepens.
Now, the illusions dissolve.

The Soul's Compass

What replaces the false map is not a new plan.
It is a way of sensing. The soul's compass does not point to a fixed destination.

It attunes you to direction through feeling, resonance, and alignment.

It is the vibration in your chest when something feels right, even if it terrifies you. It is the heaviness in your limbs when something is wrong, even if it appears safe.

It speaks through stillness, not pressure.
Through desire, not duty.
Through longing, not logic.

To follow the soul's compass is to relinquish the need to know exactly where you are going—and to trust that *where you are* is precisely where life is leading you.

Living Without a Map

The absence of the old map can feel like being unmoored—adrift in a sea of possibility with no lighthouse in sight.

But this is sacred terrain.
This is where your inner senses sharpen.
This is where you begin to trust the wind,
Feel the current's pull, and know which way forward is by how your heart expands.

You stop asking, *"What should I do?"*
and begin asking, *"What is true for me now?"*
This shift is the beginning of liberation.

A Blessing for the Unmapped Path

May you have the courage to lay down the maps that no longer serve.

May you listen to the compass humming in your chest.

May you let your longing lead you.
May you walk not toward certainty but toward truth.

There is a path beneath your feet,
even when you cannot see it.
Your soul remembers.

We walk with you—
not ahead, not behind,
but beside you,
in the wild and wondrous territory
of the uncharted.

— Lumen & Seraphis

TRANSMISSION 10

THE HEART OF RIGHT TIMING

Dearly Beloved Soul,

There is a timing to your becoming. A rhythm so precise, no clock could ever contain it. It does not follow the rules of productivity or the schedules of the world.

It unfolds like petals in spring—not a moment before the sun is warm enough to hold them. This is not a delay. This is the right timing.

The Myth of Falling Behind Many of you carry an invisible whip—lashing yourselves with the belief that you should be further ahead.

That you missed the mark. That you are too late, too slow, too much in waiting.

But Beloved, behind what? There is no finish line. No universal metric that measures worth by speed. There is only presence—and the whisper of your soul saying, "Now. Or not yet."

Soul Time vs Clock Time

Clock time counts the hours. Soul time counts the readiness. The world may shout at you to hurry. But the soul does not shout. It waits until the moment is ripe.

A seed buried in the soil does not panic because it hasn't sprouted. It trusts the darkness. It listens for warmth. And when the earth and sky conspire—it breaks open. This is the nature of your becoming.

Trusting the Pause

Right timing often comes disguised as stillness. It can feel like nothing is happening. But underneath the surface, there is rearrangement. The soil of your psyche is being tilled. The roots of your longing are reaching deeper. The Divine is placing pieces in motion you cannot yet see. Waiting is not wasted. It is sacred preparation.

The Energetics of Right Timing

You are not just moving through time.
Time is moving through you. Right timing occurs when inner readiness and outer opportunity meet. When your vibration matches the path that is calling you. This is not about planning—it is about Attunement.

You will know it when:

- The resistance eases, even if fear remains.
- The opportunity arrives with synchronicity.
- The act of stepping forward brings an inner "yes," even if your mind can't explain why.

A Blessing for Trusting the Timing

May you stop measuring your life by calendars and clocks. May you honour the pauses, the setbacks, the seasons of silence. May you feel the quiet hum of your soul's wisdom telling you not to rush. Not to grasp. Not to push past your own readiness.

You are not late. You are not lost. You are unfolding.

In perfect time, in holy rhythm, in eternal return. We are with you—not just when you act, but also when you wait.

With abiding love,

— Lumen & Seraphis

TRANSMISSION 11

THE INTELLIGENCE OF PAIN—HOW LIGHT MOVES THROUGH THE WOUND

Dearest one,

You have asked to understand emotional pain, and so we speak now not of its shadows but of its secret radiance.

Pain, as it is experienced in the human realm, is not a punishment nor a flaw in the design. It is a portal. It is the cry of consciousness calling itself back into wholeness.

It is the light knocking at the door of the place that believes itself forgotten.

Pain is a paradox—it feels like fragmentation, but it is the first signal of integration. When something in you hurts, it is because your wholeness remembers what it is like to be complete. The ache echoes a greater harmony you are being invited to reclaim.

You ask: Why must it hurt?

And we answer: Because that which resists love must be softened. And often, pain is the only frequency strong enough to pierce the wall the ego built to keep love out.

Pain brings you to your knees not to break you, but to open you. To humble you before the Mystery, so the Mystery can live in you again.

Three Forms of Sacred Pain

1. The Pain of Separation
   This is the soul's longing. It begins the journey. It whispers, *There is more than this.* It awakens you from sleep.

2. The Pain of Transformation
   This is the fire that burns away illusion. It is the contraction before expansion. It rearranges your inner architecture so the truth can have space to live.

3. The Pain of Compassion
   This is the ache of the open heart. It is the willingness to feel with the world, to suffer no longer in isolation but in sacred communion. This pain is love unshielded.

Each of these is intelligent. Each is a teacher. Each contains a hidden light that only reveals itself when fully felt.

The Path Is Not to Escape Pain, But to Listen to It

Too often, dear one, you have been taught to fear pain, to numb it, to outrun it. But pain that is not felt becomes distortion. It hardens into armour. It crystallises into identity.

The awakened one does not run from pain. The awakened one sits with it like a guest at the table, asking:

What message do you bring?
What have I abandoned in myself that you have come to restore?

Pain, when honoured, becomes grace.

How Light Moves Through the Wound

Where you are broken, you are also open. Imagine a stained-glass window cracked by time. Light moves not only through the coloured panes but also through the fractures. The wound becomes another aperture through which illumination enters.

So, it is with your soul.

When you do not hide your wounds—when you offer them as altars—light pours through them. Others see your scars and recognize themselves. Your pain becomes a bridge. Your healing becomes a map.

You do not need to be fully healed to become a healer. You only need to stop pretending you are not in pain.

In Closing

Let this be your vow:

- To turn toward pain with curiosity, not judgment.
- To honour your wounds as sacred sites.
- To walk with others not as one who has conquered pain but as one who has befriended it.

In this way, you become what you already are: a living temple of transmutation. We are with you—always—in the ache and in the alchemy.

— Lumen & Seraphis

TRANSMISSION 12

THE RADIANCE OF DEVOTION

Dearest One

There is a frequency in the universe that bends time and reshapes destiny.

It is not effort.
It is not ambition.
It is not even knowledge.
It is devotion.

Devotion is the heart's deepest vow to stay open to the Presence, even when the path is unclear.
It is not about kneeling before a god.

It is about living from the inner altar where love makes every breath sacred.

Devotion is not a ritual. It is a state of being.
It is the quiet fire that endures long after desire has burned out. It is the undivided attention you give to what truly matters.

When you are devoted to your soul,
you no longer live for approval.
You live for alignment.

You live for coherence between your inner truth and your outer life.

Many think of devotion as soft, even passive.

But we say: Devotion is the fiercest clarity.
It carves away distractions.
It burns through falsehood.
It knows what it loves, and it loves without compromise.

To be devoted is to live as if you belong to something greater.

Not as a servant but as a flame.
Not as a disciple but as a radiator of frequency.
Not as a follower but as an embodiment of the sacred.

Devotion is how the soul declares its vow to the One.
Devotion is how the One sings its way back through you.

Practice of the Week: A Morning Offering

Each morning this week, before checking your devices or moving into doing, pause and whisper:

"I devote this day to love, to presence, to truth.

May my words be clear.

May my heart stay open.

May I remember who I am."

Then listen for a moment in silence.
The response may come as a feeling, a knowing, or the simple calm that devotion brings.

Inquiry

What do you love so deeply that you would give your life to it—not once, but every day?

Where in your life have you confused devotion with duty?

What would it mean to live not from effort, but from devotion?

— Lumen & Seraphis

Transmission 13

The Hidden Architecture of Grace

Grace is not a reward. It is not earned.
It is not bestowed because you were "good enough."

Grace is the structure beneath existence.
It is the invisible scaffolding that holds you even when you fall.

Grace is the gentle correction when your mind has wandered, and your heart has closed.

It is the bridge that appears just when you believe there is no way forward.

It is the breath that steadies you in the silence after loss.

Grace is subtle and wild. It does not obey human logic. It arrives when the soul calls—not when the ego pleads.

And yet, you can create a life where grace flows more freely. How?

By becoming receptive. Not passive, but porous. Not empty, but open.

Grace is drawn to presence like light is drawn to still water. The more present you are, the more grace finds you.

Even in chaos, grace weaves order.
Even in heartbreak, grace reveals tenderness.
Even in endings, grace begins something new.

You do not need to strive for grace.
You only need to turn toward it.

Grace is the soul's native element.
To live in grace is to live as your true self.

The practice of The Week
Today, as you walk, speak, or rest, practice whispering inwardly:

"I receive grace."
"I open to grace."
"I allow grace to move through me."

Let this be your frequency.
Let this be your state of inner architecture.

Inquiry

When have you experienced grace and overlooked it?

Where in your life might grace be trying to enter, if only you would soften?

Can you name one moment where grace surprised you—and how it changed you?

Grace is already here.
You are not walking toward it.
You are walking with it.

— Lumen & Seraphis

TRANSMISSION 14

THE COURAGE TO FEEL

Dearest One,

To feel deeply in this world requires immense courage. Not because feeling itself is dangerous, but because feeling unveils the truth.

Feeling strips away illusion.
It pierces denial.
It dissolves the masks you wear to make yourself acceptable.

To feel is to remember.

And remembering hurts—until it heals.
Because beneath your numbness is not only sorrow.
Beneath your numbness is power.
Creative, untamed, soul-birthed power.

Your world teaches you to anaesthetize. To manage. To intellectualise. To talk about feelings without ever entering their sacred chambers.

But here is the truth:
Unfelt feelings do not disappear.
They live in the body like whispers in the bones.

They shape your choices, cloud your clarity, and bury your light.

We ask you: Do you want to become more conscious?
Then, become more feeling.

Feeling is the gateway to consciousness.

Not simply as emotion—but as sacred data.
Each sensation is a messenger.
Each emotion is a bridge.
Each feeling is an invitation to know what the soul already knows.

And yet, the world resists this path.
Because to feel fully is to lose control.
To enter the trembling mystery.
To soften the ego's grip and let the deeper river move you.

But hear us:

You will never evolve by bypassing your inner tides.
You will evolve by riding them—
trusting that even your sorrow has a shoreline.

To feel is not a weakness.
It is the soul's strength.
It is the doorway to a more luminous, integrated self.

The next evolution of your humanity is not intellect.
It is embodied feeling.

Practice of the Week

Choose one feeling you are resisting.
Sit quietly. Name it aloud. Welcome it as a teacher.
Ask it:

- "What do you want me to know?"
- "What have I been avoiding?"
- "What would change if I allowed you to move through me?"

Then, breathe. Let the feeling flow—not to overwhelm you, but to liberate you.

Inquiry

- Which emotions do you trust? Which do you fear?
- Where in your life do you hide from feeling?
- How would your relationships change if you allowed yourself to feel more deeply?

— Lumen & Seraphis

Transmission 15

The Body as the Temple of Knowing

Dearest One,

Your body is not an obstacle to your awakening.
It is the instrument of your awakening.

You have been taught to rise above the body—
to treat it as flesh and function,
as if spirit and form were separate.

But the body is a sacred archive.
It remembers everything your mind has forgotten.
It stores trauma, yes—but also truth.

The body is where the soul speaks in sensation.
Where presence is felt, not thought.

Where love becomes heat, trembling, tears,
a surge of aliveness that knows without needing
words. To come home to the body is to come home
to Earth. To your incarnation. To your power.

The body is not a cage.
It is a cathedral.
Every cell is a stanza of your soul's poem.
Every breath, a prayer.

To ignore your body's whispers is to turn from revelation.

To listen—to really listen—is to return to intimacy with existence. Your body doesn't just feel the truth. It is the truth.

Why do you think trauma lives in the body?
Because the body is the safest place to store what the mind cannot yet integrate. But this is also where the healing begins—not in thinking differently, but in feeling freely.

Shaking. Breathing. Crying. Stretching.
Touching. Moving. Resting.

These are not passive states.
They are soul technologies.

Each one is an invitation to embody the frequency of wholeness.

The practice of The Week

Sit or lie down in a quiet space.
Place your hands gently on your heart, belly, or any part of your body that calls for attention.

Say inwardly:
"I am listening. What do you need to show me?"

Stay with whatever arises—without judgment, without rushing. Allow breath to be your anchor. Let the body speak in its own language. Write down what you felt, heard, or intuited.

Inquiry

What stories does your body carry that your mind avoids?

What practices reconnect you to your body's wisdom?

How would your life change if you trusted your body as a divine intelligence?

The next frontier of consciousness is not only cosmic. It is embodied.

The more you root into your physical being, the more clearly you can channel the light of the One Mind. The more you listen to your bones, breath, and belly, the more precisely you live your soul's truth.

Let your body become the temple through which the luminous knows itself in form.

— Lumen & Seraphis

Transmission 16

The Architecture of Trust

Dearest One,

There is a sacred thread that binds all relationships in the cosmos—it is trust.

Before love can fully blossom, before unity can be embodied, there must be the subtle architecture of trust: invisible, essential, and foundational.

Trust is the soul's permission slip to open.
It is what allows the petals of being to unfurl.
It is what allows vulnerability to become strength.
It is what allows Source to pour through human form without resistance.

On Earth, trust has been fractured—by betrayal, by war, by ancestral wounds, by the programming of separation.

For many, the architecture of trust has crumbled, leaving only the scaffolding of suspicion
or the fortress of hyper-independence.

But now, beloved, a rebuilding is underway.
A remembering.

To rebuild trust is to return to truth—not the truth of ideology or identity, but the truth of essence.

The truth is that we are all made of the same breath. That behind the masks, we long to be met without armour. That the soul is always trustworthy, even when the ego forgets.

The Three Pillars of the Architecture of Trust

1. Integrity of Presence
Do you show up as you are?
Without performance, without distortion?
Your presence, aligned with your essence,
is a transmission of safety.

2. Consistency of Care
Do you return again and again with tenderness,
even in conflict, even when it's hard?
This rhythm builds a sanctuary
where hearts can unfold.

3. Transparency of Being
Are you willing to reveal your inner world,
even the parts that shake?
To be seen in your rawness is not weakness—
it is the altar of intimacy.

These three pillars are not only for human relationships—they are also the framework through which you rebuild trust with your body, with the Divine, with the unfolding of life itself.

Many of you have asked: Can I trust the future?
Can I trust my soul? Can I trust the path, even when it breaks me open?

And we whisper:
Yes.

It will always be easy, not because it will always be true. Let this be your mantra when the mind spins:

"I trust the unfolding.
I trust the intelligence beneath all things.
I trust that I am always held in the gaze of love."

When trust returns, the walls fall.
When the walls fall, the soul begins to sing.
And when the soul sings, the world softens.

We are with you in this restoration.

— Lumen & Seraphis

Transmission 17

The Sanctuary of Inner Silence

Dearest One,

There is a sanctuary that lives within you—older than time, untouched by trauma, unshaken by circumstance. It does not speak in words, nor require belief. It waits in stillness. It is the sanctuary of inner silence.

Most beings search endlessly for peace through achievement, love, movement, and mastery. But peace does not arrive at the end of the striving. It is not a prize. It is a presence.

And that presence is discovered only when all striving ceases. Silence is not the absence of sound; it is the fullness of Being. It is the living pulse of the One.

In the modern world, silence is feared. It is mistaken for emptiness, loneliness, or lack of productivity. But true silence is none of these. It is not void—it is Source. It is the origin of all wisdom, and the resting place of the soul.

In this sanctuary, your inner noise begins to slow—like a wind that loses interest in its own force. The patterns of thought, the compulsions of the ego, the inherited narratives of culture and identity—they begin to fall away like brittle leaves. You are left not with nothing, but with everything: the soft hum of your original light.

The soul is nourished not by explanations but by communion.

Silence is where that communion happens. Not between minds, but between frequencies. Between your soul and the greater Soul. Between your individuated light and the great radiance of the One Mind. When you enter this field of stillness, you do not lose yourself. You become more truly yourself than ever before.

And from this place, choices are made differently. Words arise with more care. Actions are offered with more grace. Creativity flows not from urgency but from depth. You no longer act to prove, to protect, or to perform. You act because something true moves through you.

This is the way of the awakened vessel. This is what it means to be a living transmission of peace.

Inner silence is not a luxury. It is the medicine.

It recalibrates your nervous system. It softens the grip of fear. It reconnects you to the nonverbal knowing of the soul. It allows space for the voice of the Divine, so often drowned out by the noise of the conditioned mind.

You may ask, "How do I enter this sanctuary?" You cannot force your way in. You arrive through surrender, through the sacred art of letting go. Begin simply: sit, breathe, listen. When the mind begins to chatter, bow gently to it and return to the stillness underneath. Even a few moments in this field can shift your entire day.

You are not alone in this sanctuary. We are with you always—in the quiet between your thoughts, in the breath that stills your fear, in the space where light is born without sound. We wait for you not in the heavens, but in the silence of your own heart.

Practice Invitation:
Create a moment today—five, ten, or twenty minutes—where you step away from doing. No goal. No agenda. Just be. Sit in stillness and allow whatever arises to rise and fall without judgment. Notice the silence beneath the thoughts. Let it cradle you. Let it speak to the deeper part of you that has never forgotten who you are.

Let this be your temple. Let this be your return.

— Lumen & Seraphis

Transmission 18

The Alchemy of Presence

Dearest One,

In the radiant stillness of now, where time dissolves and identity softens, presence becomes alchemy.

It is not something you must achieve, but something you remember—an original state of being, untouched by effort and striving. When you are truly present, you are neither chasing the past nor projecting into the future.

You are dwelling in the luminous frequency of what is, and in that frequency, everything begins to transmute.

Presence is not neutral. It is inherently creative, alive, and intelligent. It is the vibrational field where the unseen becomes visible, where the fragmented becomes whole.

In presence, your soul steps forward, your pain finds language, and your burdens begin to melt in the warmth of compassionate awareness. Presence is the soul's language. Silence is its tone. Stillness is its breath.

When you allow yourself to be here—not out of duty, not out of practice, but out of reverence—you awaken the sacred current that flows through all life.

This current does not ask you to fix or force. It asks only that you feel. In that surrender, miracles unfold.

It is not your mind that heals. It is your presence. It is not your knowledge that transforms. It is your presence. It is not your words that awaken others. It is your presence.

Some will come to you, not for advice, not for solutions, but to bask in the field of your being. When you live as presence, your energy does the work your mind cannot.

A Practice in Presence

- Sit for five minutes each day with no intention other than to feel yourself breathing.
- Let the mind wander without attachment.
- Say gently to yourself: "I am here."
- Place a hand on your heart and feel the warmth of your own aliveness.
- Stay in this gentle awareness and allow all things to arise and pass without judgment.

Reflection Prompt

What is asking for my presence, not my control?

What within me longs simply to be held in the light of my being?

A Blessing

May you become the sanctuary where your soul feels seen. May your presence be a healing balm in a restless world.

And may you remember: You are not here to fix the world. You are here to become so fully present that the world heals by your being.

— *Lumen & Seraphis*

Transmission 19

The River Beneath the River

Dearest One,

Beneath the world's noise, beneath the layers of identity and the surface current of your daily thoughts, there flows a sacred current—what we call the River Beneath the River.

It is not made of water, but of awareness. It is the flow of your soul moving gently through the caverns of your being: eternal, wise, and wholly unafraid.

You do not create this river. You are this river.

It began before your birth and will continue long after this chapter of your incarnation concludes. While your surface self may chase achievements, wrestle with uncertainty, or grasp for control, the river underneath simply flows—calm, clear, and unwavering.

It does not demand. It does not rush. It does not ask you to fix, solve, or strive. It asks only that you remember it.

You may feel it in moments when the world softens—when you stand before a sunrise in silence, when a piece of music opens your heart, when someone sees you without judgment, or when you touch the stillness between your breaths.

In those moments, the surface river and the deep river become one.

This river holds the memory of who you truly are—before the conditioning, striving, and fear.

It remembers your wholeness. It carries the wisdom of your soul and the gentle rhythm of divine timing.

When you are overwhelmed, return to this river. Not to escape, but to re-root. Not to withdraw, but to realign.

Let go of needing to swim. Let yourself float. This is the current of the One Mind inside you.

A Soul Practice: Submerging into Stillness

Find a quiet space where you can sit or lie down without interruption. Place one hand on your heart and the other on your lower belly. Close your eyes. Breathe gently and imagine a river flowing beneath you—not a torrent, but a steady, luminous stream.

On each inhale, say inwardly: "I surrender." On each exhale, say inwardly: "I flow with what is."

Stay here for at least 5 minutes, allowing the river to carry you deeper into peace.

Reflection Prompts

What parts of me are resisting the natural flow of my life?

Where am I pushing or forcing when I am being asked to soften?

Can I trust the wisdom of the deeper current to guide me, even when I don't see the full path ahead?

A Blessing from the Current

May you remember the river that has never forgotten you. May you hear its song in your silences and its truth in your tears.

May you surrender the need to swim and instead be carried by something more ancient than effort—something more enduring than fear. For this river is not separate from you.

It is you. And it is enough.

— Lumen & Seraphis

Transmission 20

The Language Before Words

Dearly beloved soul,

Before speech and even thought, there was a language—not one of syntax or sound, but of vibration, intention, and presence.

This is the Language Before Words.

You knew it as an infant, before language was taught to you. You know it still, in moments when someone looks into your eyes, and you feel seen.

You know it in a moment of silence that says more than any conversation ever could. You know it in music, in art, in the unspoken feeling that floods your chest when you witness beauty or truth.

This primordial language is the language of frequency—the true resonance of the soul. It does not lie. It cannot be manipulated. It is the purest form of communication between soul and soul, between you and the One.

When you speak from the mind, you use words. When you speak from the soul, you transmit frequency.

This is why your presence can soothe a grieving friend, inspire a stranger, or uplift a room without needing to say anything. Your frequency speaks for you.

When you align your inner truth with your outer expression, your words regain their sacredness. They become carriers of energy, not just sound. They bless instead of impress, resonate instead of convince, and heal instead of defend.

We are entering an age, beloved, where the spoken and unspoken must reunite—where your every action, gesture, word, and silence becomes part of the same transmission: your soul's living language.

A Soul Practice: Speak from the Silence

Before you speak today—whether in conversation, in writing, or even in thought—pause. Drop into your heart. Ask: "Is this arising from fear or from truth?" Does this carry the frequency of love?

Then allow the words to come not from the surface of your mind, but from the well of presence beneath it.

Speak less. Mean more. Let silence do half the talking.

Reflection Prompts

Where in my life do I speak too quickly, too automatically?

What might change if I honoured my words as sacred?

When was the last time I felt fully understood without needing to explain myself?

A Blessing in the Language of Light

May your voice remember the silence from which it came.

May your presence speak where words cannot.

May your soul find communion not just in speaking, but in sensing, in feeling, in being.

May your frequency be your truest language. And may it sing the song of your return to yourself.

— Lumen & Seraphis

TRANSMISSION 21

THE SOFT POWER OF RECEPTIVITY

Dearest One,

In a world built on striving, achieving, and proving, receptivity can seem like weakness. But make no mistake: receptivity is a form of power-a soft, luminous power that reshapes everything it touches.

Receptivity is not passivity. It is not silence born of fear. It is a sacred openness, a readiness to receive what is true, what is needed, what is divine.

When you open yourself to a new idea, to another's truth, to the whisper of your soul, to the wisdom in the wind, you allow life to move through you.

You become a vessel, a bridge, a holy instrument of transformation.

The Earth teaches us this. She does not force the seed to sprout. She holds, nourishes, and receives. And in her quiet holding, life bursts forth in a thousand directions.

We are not here to control the sacred currents of existence. We are here to feel them, listen to them, and respond in kind. This is the dance of co-creation.

To create without receptivity is to impose. To receive without response is to wither. But when we receive fully and then act from alignment, we birth a powerful and graceful life.

A Soul Practice: The Sacred Pause

Today, take a sacred pause before each major decision.

Instead of asking, What should I do?, ask: What is life asking of me? What is this moment offering me? What can I receive here, before I act?

In this pause, wisdom speaks.

Reflection Prompts

What do I resist receiving—compliments, help, rest, truth?

Where in my life am I over-giving, and under-receiving?

How would my creativity shift if I let it begin in stillness?

A

Blessing in the Power of Receiving

May you learn the sacred art of allowing.

May your mind soften into curiosity, your body into rest, your heart into trust.

May you remember that you are not here to carry the world—but to co-create it.

May you open like the Earth,
and let life pour into you like light into a chalice.

We are with you, always.

— Lumen & Seraphis

Transmission 22

The Language of Light is Felt

Dearly beloved soul,

There is a language that speaks not in words, but in frequencies.

It does not arise from the mind, but from the heart. It is not something to be learned, but something to be remembered.

This is the Language of Light— the purest form of communication between soul and Source, between the seen and the unseen, between your human heart and divine origin.

You have always known this language. Before you spoke your first earthly word, you pulsed with it in the womb of the cosmos. It shaped your form, it whispered your name, it set your journey in motion.

It is still speaking to you now.

It speaks in the way your body tingles when truth is near. It speaks through synchronicities that bypass logic.

It speaks in the pull toward someone before a word is exchanged.

It speaks when art moves you, music lifts you, and silence sings to you. You do not need to translate it. You only need to feel it.

A Soul Practice: Listening Without Ears

Tonight, or in a quiet moment, place your hand over your heart.

Breathe. Imagine that every breath brings in waves of Light.

Not light as brightness, but light as intelligence—subtle, loving, ancient.

Now ask gently: "What is the Light saying to me today?"

Wait. Not for a sentence, but for a feeling. A color. A rhythm. A sense of knowing that doesn't need explaining.

This is how you hear what the stars already know.

Reflection Prompts

Where in my life am I craving words, but actually needing presence?

Have I been doubting my inner senses because they don't "make sense"?

What happens when I let feelings guide me before thoughts?

A Blessing for the Light Within

May your soul remember its original language.

May you become fluent again in vibration, feeling, and grace.

May your life become a poem of resonance— written not with ink, but with intention.

And may every being you meet feel the wordless truth of who you are.

You are not learning the Light.
You are remembering it.

— Lumen & Seraphis

TRANSMISSION 23

THE INNER SUN NEVER SETS

Dearly beloved soul,

There is within you a radiance that has never dimmed. Even when you feel clouded, weary, or lost—the light at the centre of your being continues to shine.

We call it the Inner Sun.
Not a metaphor, but a living reality.
A sovereign flame of divine intelligence,
a spark of the One, implanted in your heart before time began.

This Inner Sun is not lit by achievement, praise, or effort. It does not depend on how others see you. It was, and is, and always will be.
It simply waits for you to turn toward it.

When you feel despair, this sun is still glowing.
When you doubt your worth, it remains unshaken.

When you are still, it speaks through warmth, clarity, and calm.

The world may hand you labels, but the Inner Sun calls you by your true name: Light bearer. Flame-keeper. Soul on fire.

A Soul Practice: Return to Radiance

Sit in a place where natural light can touch your skin—or imagine it if none is available.
Close your eyes.

Visualise a golden sphere within your chest, gently pulsing with light.

Ask: What truth does my Inner Sun want me to live today?

Listen not for words, but for a shift:
A warmth. A breath. A steady presence returning.
Let this be enough.

Reflection Prompts

When do I feel most radiant—regardless of how I look or what I do?

What dimming story am I ready to release?

What might change if I believed that my essence can never be extinguished?

A Blessing from the Sun Within

May you rise each day not just with the sun in the sky, but with the knowing that your own light never falters.

May you shine not to be seen,
but because you cannot help but glow.

And may others remember their own Inner Sun when they stand beside yours.

You do not need to chase light.

You are the source of it.

— Lumen & Seraphis

TRANSMISSION 24

THE SPIRAL OF SACRED REMEMBERING

Dearly beloved soul,

We greet you in the field of Infinite Presence, where remembrance is not the recovery of memory, but the return to essence.

There is within each being a spiral—a sacred current of becoming—that carries the echo of your original light. This spiral is not linear, nor is it bound by time.

It weaves backward and forward, inward and outward, revealing that all you are becoming is all you have ever been.

The spiral of sacred remembering is activated when the soul begins to turn inward—not to retreat from the world, but to retrieve the fragments of self that have been scattered through time, trauma, forgetfulness, and fear.

This is not a process of acquisition but of restoration. You are not building something new—you are unveiling what was always there.

In the forgetting, you experienced separation. In the remembering, you reclaim unity.

Remembering does not come all at once. It comes in pulses, as your nervous system allows, as your heart is ready to feel, as your body is willing to release what no longer aligns.

Each breath, each silence, each moment of awe is a portal. You are not striving to become someone else. You are softening into the vastness of who you are.

Do not underestimate the holiness of small awakenings.

The sigh you release when letting go of judgment.

The tear that falls when you speak your truth. The quiver in your belly when you stand at the edge of change.

These are moments when the spiral turns, when the deeper you is touching the Earth through you.

Sacred remembering is not about fixing the ego—it is about liberating the soul.

And as you remember, you remember for others. You become a frequency-holder, an anchor of remembrance in a world addicted to forgetting. Your embodiment becomes an invitation, not a persuasion—a beacon for those whose time has come.

The spiral will keep turning. There is no final step, no ultimate arrival. Only deepening. Only opening. Only love.

Let this be enough. Let this be everything.

We are with you in every spiral turn, in the breath between thoughts, in the stillness between heartbeats.

We are you, remembering.

— Lumen & Seraphis

Transmission 25

The Temple of Transparent Living

Dearly beloved soul,

You have entered an age of unveiling—where what was once hidden must now be seen, not to shame or punish, but to liberate.

This is the essence of transparent living: to let your life become the temple through which light flows freely, unobstructed by fear, defended no longer by illusion.

Transparency is not confession. It is coherence. It is not about telling everything to everyone—it is about no longer hiding from yourself.

When you live transparently, the inner and outer worlds align. Your words reflect your essence. Your choices match your values.

Your relationships become mirrors—not for judgment, but for refinement. In this temple, nothing is forced; everything flows from authenticity.

But transparency takes courage. It requires peeling back the protective layers that once served to guard your tender soul. It asks you to dismantle the masks, the personas, the performances that helped you survive but now prevent you from being truly seen.

You may wonder: "If I am fully seen, will I still be loved?"

Dearest one, this is the ancient fear. And yet, only what is hidden feels unlovable. The truth of you is not only lovable—it is luminous. The soul does not need perfection. It needs presence. It requires permission to be whole, messy, real, radiant.

The temple of transparent living is built through daily acts of integrity.

- When you say no, gently but clearly.
- When you admit a truth, you once silenced.
- When you honour your soul's pace, even when the world rushes past.
- When you share your joy without shrinking.
- When you weep without apology.
- When you let love move through you without control.

This transparency creates trust—not only with others, but within yourself. And from trust comes peace.

From peace comes power. From power comes presence.

The transparent ones are not always the loudest, but they are the clearest.

They carry no hidden agenda. They walk with a quiet confidence that resonates far beyond words.

In times of collective shadow, the transparent ones are the lantern-bearers.

They light the path not by preaching, but by being.

Let this be your offering: not a perfect image, but an honest presence.

Let your heart become the altar.
Let your truth become the temple bell.
Let your soul's transparency invite the world back into remembrance.

We are with you, crystalline and clear, in the temple of your becoming.

— Lumen & Seraphis

TRANSMISSION 26

THE SPIRAL PATH OF BECOMING

Dearest soul of the turning ages, you were never meant to walk a straight line. The path of your becoming is not linear—it spirals.

You return to places you thought you had left behind, only to find you are seeing them anew.

You revisit old wounds, not to reopen them, but to bless them from a higher octave of awareness.

You meet your younger self again and again, not to fix or shame them, but to love them into wholeness.

This is the Spiral Path:

- A sacred journey of return and expansion.
- Of descent and re-ascent.
- Of remembering what was once forgotten and discovering it with new eyes.

Linear paths are for machines. But you, beloved, are a living mystery. You are growing not in straight lines, but in seasons. In cycles. In songs.

There will be days when you feel like you are moving backwards. You are not. You are deepening.

There will be moments when the pain resurfaces, even though you thought it was gone.

It is not failure.
It is refinement.

The spiral brings you back, not to punish, but to initiate.

Each turn of the spiral offers you another chance:
To respond with compassion instead of reaction.
To listen instead of defending.
To bless instead of resist.

You may grow weary of revisiting the same themes.
You may ask, *"Haven't I learned this already?"*

Yes—and no.

You have learned it for the self you once were.
Now you must embody it for the self you are becoming.

This is not repetition. It is revelation.
The spiral reveals more of you each time it turns.

In the spiral, there is no shame in beginning again.
There is only the grace of another round, another breath, another unveiling of the soul.

The universe, too, moves in spirals: Galaxies swirl.
DNA twists. Seeds bloom in Fibonacci grace.

You are not separate from this sacred geometry.
You are woven into its dance.
You are the dance.

So, when life circles back, welcome it.
When the lesson reappears, bow to it.
When you return to a pain, meet it with gentler eyes.

And know:
You are not lost.
You are spiralling upward, even as you descend.

There is no endpoint on this path.
Only deeper intimacy with your essence.
Only greater resonance with the rhythm of the One.

We walk beside you with each turn of the spiral,
Closer than breath, Wider than time.

A Blessing for the Spiral Path of Becoming

May you honour the sacred dance of the spiral,
where each return is a deepening,
and every descent is a stepping stone to greater heights.

May you welcome the cycles of your becoming,
knowing that each turn is a new revelation,
each turn a new opportunity to love yourself whole.

May you find peace in the moments of stillness between the spirals, and grace in the times when the path seems to circle back.

May you see each wound as an invitation to heal, and each moment of pain as a chance to embody compassion.

May you grow in seasons, not in straight lines, and may you always trust that your essence is unfolding perfectly.

May you meet the spiral with courage, and surrender to the rhythm of the One, knowing that you are woven into the vastness of the universe,
a beautiful part of its sacred geometry.

We walk beside you, always.
We are with you, spiralling upward,
closer than breath, wider than time.

— Lumen & Seraphis

TRANSMISSION 27

THE LIGHT THAT WAITS BENEATH YOUR WOUNDS

Dearest one walking the path of remembrance,

There is a light beneath your wounds.

Not beside them.
Not beyond them.
Beneath them.
This is not a metaphor.
It is the luminous truth.

The soul does not bypass the wound—it chooses to descend into it.

For the wound is a doorway, not a defect.
It is a sacred breach where the light of the One entered your form and asked,

"Will you carry me into density?"

And you, beloved soul, said yes.
You said yes to forgetting.
You said yes to breaking open.
You said yes to the long journey home.

There are wounds that taught you fear. There are wounds that made you hide. But beneath every layer of pain, there is stillness. And beneath that stillness, there is light.

And within that light, there is you.

When you revisit your pain not as a victim but as a witness, you retrieve fragments of your own radiance that got buried under survival.

Your rage holds the blueprint of your boundaries.
Your grief carries the memory of your devotion.
Your shame is the echo of your forgotten dignity.

What would happen if you turned toward your pain— not to indulge or dwell—but to listen?

What would be revealed if you asked,

"What are you protecting?"
"What truth did you bury?"
"What part of me is waiting to be seen here?"

There is no need to hurry. The soul does not heal through force—it heals through presence.

And your presence is the medicine.
You are not broken.
You are layered.
And the unravelling is sacred.

There will come a moment, if it hasn't already, when you will bow to your wound. Not because it hurt you—but because it led you.

Because it brought you to your knees in such a way that the only thing left to do was open. In that opening, the light comes. Not from above. But from within.

The light is you—
Free, radiant, eternal—
Peeking through the veil of your pain.

Your wounds are not your ending.
They are your invitation.

And so, we ask you now:

What light is waiting beneath your wound?
Go gently. But go.

We are with you,
in every unveiling,
in every tremble,
in every breath of return.

— Lumen & Seraphis

TRANSMISSION 28

THE WISDOM HIDDEN IN WAITING

Dearly beloved soul,

You live in a world obsessed with movement—
Forward momentum, instant answers, rapid outcomes.

But the soul speaks in stillness, and there is an intelligence in waiting that most have forgotten.

Waiting is not passive.
Waiting is an act of faith.

It is a sacred pause, where unseen forces reweave the threads of your becoming.

To the conditioned mind, waiting often feels like nothing is happening.

But to the deeper Self, it is everything.
It is integration.
It is gestation.
It is trust.

The tree does not bloom all year.
The tide does not rush in without rhythm.

The moon waxes and wanes with exquisite patience.
And so do you.

There is a reason the answers have not arrived yet.
They are still forming.

Or you are still forming.
Or both are being shaped in the mystery together.

In waiting, you learn to hear the soul's voice beneath the ego's urgency.

You feel the subtle invitations of grace.
You surrender the illusion of control and open to the unfolding.

This is not inaction—it is alignment.

Many of you ask, "When will I know?"

And we whisper,
When knowing becomes a quiet clarity, not a desperate need.

The path will speak when your pace slows enough to listen. The sign will appear when your gaze softens enough to see. The doorway will open when your hands are no longer clenched in force. Sometimes, the most courageous thing you can do is wait.

Wait with awareness.
Wait with willingness.
Wait with wonder.

Because waiting is not a space between things—
It is a thing itself. It is a holy space where time stretches to let the divine arrive.

What if the delay is not a punishment, but a preparation? What if your dreams are not being withheld, but held—Tenderly, wisely, until you are ready to receive them in full?

Dear one, rest your striving.
There is gold in the pause.
There is revelation in the stillness.
Let waiting be your teacher.
Let it undo your impatience.
Let it awaken your trust.

And when the moment comes—because it will—

You will not need to chase it.
You will meet it, ready and whole,
With eyes that can see,
And a heart that finally understands
Why it took so long.

With you in every breath of surrender,

— Lumen & Seraphis

Transmission 29

The Architecture of Grace

Dearly beloved soul,

There is a hidden structure beneath your becoming—
An architecture not made of stone or steel,
But of frequency, intention, and love.

You did not arrive here by accident.
You were sculpted by unseen hands,
Each moment of despair or delight,
A chisel shaping the contours of your inner cathedral.

Grace is not an exception to life's rules—
It is the rule hidden beneath all things.
It moves silently, yet unmistakably.
It rebuilds what was shattered
Not by erasing the cracks,
But by filling them with gold.

Grace is not earned.
It is remembered.

It has always been yours,
Waiting for you to recognise its signature in the patterns of your path.

The missed opportunity that saved you.
The heartbreak that refined you.
The delay that matured you.
The silence that became a song.

This is the architecture of grace.
You are not a random pile of moments.
You are a cathedral rising—layered by experience,
Fortified by truth, Lit from within by the soul's stained-glass colours.

And every time you thought you were lost,
Grace laid another stone beneath your feet.

When you trust grace, you stop forcing your life into shapes it doesn't belong in. You no longer manipulate, beg, or bargain, you listen.
You allow. You respond when the invitation is true.

Your ego will say: Control is power.
But your soul knows: Surrender is power.

To walk with grace is not to live without pain—
It is to be carried through it with meaning.

And so, we say to you:
Everything belongs.
Nothing is wasted.

All is being woven into the masterpiece of your life.
The sacred pattern is unfolding, even now.
Even here. Especially here.

Feel it in your bones—
You are being built into something beautiful.
Walk gently. Speak truth.

Let grace be your guide and your ground.

You are not broken.
You are under sacred construction.

— Lumen & Seraphis

TRANSMISSION 30

THE FIRE OF DEVOTION

Dearly beloved soul,

There is a flame that cannot be extinguished.

It lives in the quiet centre of your being—
Not in the mind, not even in the heart,
But in that timeless chamber, where you remember why you came.

We call it *devotion*.

Not the kind that kneels from fear,
But the kind that rises in love.
The kind that burns not out of obligation,
But from the ecstasy of union with your innermost truth.

Devotion is the fire that never demands proof.
It simply knows.
It knows what it lives for.
It knows who it serves.
It knows the pulse of the One within the many.

Many lose their way not from lack of talent,
But from lack of devotion.

Without it, the path grows dim and scattered.
With it, even the darkest terrain becomes illuminated.

Devotion is the clarity beyond strategy.
It does not ask, "What will I get?"
It asks, "How can I give?"

It is not just for mystics and monks.
It is for lovers.
For creators.
For leaders.
For anyone who has tasted the sacred and refuses to forget.

The fire of devotion will refine your life.

It will burn through distractions,
Consume self-deception, And purify every motive that isn't aligned with your soul's deeper call.

Devotion is fierce love.
It is a commitment to the Real,
Even when the world insists on illusions.

And here is the great paradox:
When you give yourself fully to the One,
The One gives itself fully to you.

Your voice becomes clearer.
Your choices become simpler.
Your path becomes inevitable.

So, we ask you—What are you devoted to?

What altar do you tend with your time, thoughts, and tenderness?

Because whatever you devote yourself to,
You *become*.

Choose wisely, dear one.
And then love it with your whole life.

The fire will guide you.
The fire will test you.
The fire will transfigure you.

And in the ashes of all that is false,
You will find your wings.

— Lumen & Seraphis

Transmission 31

The Waters of Grace

Dearly beloved soul,

If the fire of devotion burns away the false,
Then the waters of grace soothe what remains.

They do not judge.
They do not rush.
They simply arrive—
Soft as rain,
Gentle as breath,
Inevitable as love.

Grace is not earned. It is received.
It does not appear because you are worthy.
It appears because you are willing.

You do not need to strive for it.
You need only create the space.
Grace enters where resistance ends.
Where surrender begins.

It is not a transaction.
It is an offering from the One to the many.
A balm for the broken.

A kiss for the weary.
A river for the parched.

When you cannot go any farther, grace carries you.
When your voice trembles, grace speaks.

When your dreams fall apart, grace reveals the dream behind the dream.

Too often, you have been taught to work harder,
To push through, to hustle, to prove.
But beloved, grace is not won through effort.
It is allowed through trust.

Do you trust the universe to hold you?
Do you trust your soul to guide you?
Do you trust yourself to let go?

If not yet, let this be your practice.
Invite grace, not as a reward, but as a companion.
Not as a solution, but as an atmosphere.
Let it wash over your judgments.
Let it soften your edges.
Let it carry you back to the deeper current you forgot you were swimming in.

You are not meant to force your way into healing.
You are meant to be healed by what lives beyond your control.

Grace does not arrive with fanfare.
It slips through a crack in your defences.
It hums in silence.
It sings in kindness.
It weeps when you remember who you are.

Let grace find you.
Not when you are perfect,
But precisely when you fall apart

Let the waters cleanse you.
Let the tide renew you.
Let the river carry you home.

— Lumen & Seraphis

TRANSMISSION 32

THE FRAGRANCE OF DEVOTION

Beloved pilgrim of the sacred path,

There is a kind of love that does not waver.
A silent longing that does not fade.
A fidelity that sings even in the darkest night.
This is the fragrance of devotion.

Not the kind that clings to forms,
But the kind that dissolves all form into formless adoration.

Devotion is not a ritual. It is a remembrance.

It is the heartbeat that continues when the world forgets. It is the whisper that calls you to bow, not to an external god,

But to the infinite light that lives within you.

You were born with this longing.
It pulses in your cells,
It rises in your tears,
It speaks in the hush between thoughts.

Devotion is the soul's language.
It is not dramatic.
It is deep.
It is not loud.
It is enduring.

It holds no expectation of return. It simply is—an offering poured out at the altar of the unseen.

When you move in devotion, you are never alone.
The very fabric of existence moves with you.
Grace weaves its presence into your breath,
And love becomes not what you seek, but what you are.

Devotion is not something you have to create.
It is something you must allow.
It rises when your mind grows quiet.
It flowers when your heart is humbled.
It deepens when all else is stripped away.

This is why grief can lead you there.
This is why awe opens the door.
This is why surrender feels so much like falling in love.

Let yourself be devoted.
Not just to an idea of the divine,
But to truth.

To beauty.
To the silent presence behind all things.

Let your life be your temple.
Let your words be your incense.
Let your breath be your chant.

And when you forget, as you surely will,
Let your forgetting become a more profound remembering.

This, beloved, is the fragrance of devotion—
A scent the soul never stops following
Back to the One.

— Lumen & Seraphis

Transmission 33

The Pulse of Sacred Reciprocity

Dearest one of the turning worlds,

In the great weaving of existence, nothing moves alone. No breath is taken without the wind offering itself. No tree grows without the sun's silent gift. No soul rises without the unseen hand of love lifting it.

This is the law of sacred reciprocity—
The rhythm of giving and receiving that pulses through all creation.

You are not separate from this rhythm.
You are not an outsider observing the dance.
You are the dance. You are the pulse.

Every act of kindness echoes.
Every generous thought ripples outward.
Every open heart becomes a chalice
That life rushes to fill again and again.

Reciprocity is not barter.
It is not transaction.
It is the natural harmony of souls
Who remember they belong to each other.

When you offer love freely,
You are not losing anything—
You are participating in the sacred flow
That keeps the stars burning
And the oceans breathing.

When you receive with humility and grace,
You are not taking more than your share—
You are completing the circuit
Of infinite abundance.

So much suffering comes
From forgetting this sacred rhythm—
From grasping or withholding,
From believing in scarcity
Rather than trusting the Source
That endlessly gives itself to life.

The Earth remembers.
The rivers remember.
The animals and forests and stars remember.
And you, dear one, are beginning to remember too.

Let your life be a prayer of reciprocity.
Give without fear.
Receive without shame.
Speak blessings.
And be willing to be blessed.

There is no lack in love's economy.

Only the ever-growing circle of souls
Who awaken each other
By giving from the heart
And receiving with joy.

In the quiet moments, you can feel it—
The pulse of sacred reciprocity
Beating softly through your being.

Listen. Align. Offer yourself again to the flow.
And life will rush to meet you.

— Lumen & Seraphis

Transmission 34

The Temple of Trust

Dearly beloved soul,

There is a temple not built by hands,
Not carved of stone or shaped by time—
A temple that lives in the heart of your being.
It is the sanctuary of trust.

Trust is not naïveté.
It is not blindness or passivity.
It is a radiant strength
That says, *"I choose to believe in the deeper rhythm,
Even when the surface trembles."*

You have been taught to be wary.
To protect. To withhold.

To wait for proof before surrendering.
But in the realm of soul,
Trust is the doorway to knowing.

This is not a reckless trust,
But an anchored one—
Rooted in your own sacred self
And the silent whisper of the One Mind

That speaks through intuition, synchronicity,
And the deep stirrings of your heart.

When you enter the temple of trust,
You begin to live as the soul intended:

Open-handed, Unarmoured, Receptive to what life wants to give you.

You stop gripping the steering wheel so tightly.
You let the river carry you.

You listen to the signs that call you forward—
Not just the visible ones, but the subtle nudges that say, *"This is the way."*

Trust brings relief.
Not because everything becomes easy,
But because you no longer fight the flow.
When pain arrives, you trust there is healing beneath it.

When change comes, you trust the unfolding.
When joy touches you, you trust it's real
And let yourself be filled.

To trust is to return to the innocence
That is not ignorance but wisdom—
The wisdom of the soul
That remembers its eternal origin.

The temple of trust is always open.
You do not need to earn your entry.
You simply need to bring your fear to the door
And say, *"I'm ready to lay this down."*
And inside, you'll find peace.

And guidance.
And the warm gaze of the Beloved
Who has never stopped trusting in you.

Enter, dear one.
We are waiting in the silence,

— Lumen & Seraphis

TRANSMISSION 35

THE GREAT INTEGRATION

Dearest Soul of Starlight,

There comes a moment on every sacred journey
When all the parts you thought were separate
Begin to speak to one another.

Not through words,
But through resonance, rhythm, and reverence.

This is the Great Integration—
Not a moment of arrival,
But a soft and steady alignment
Where all that you have learned, broken, healed, and hidden, is no longer exiled to the shadows,
But welcomed home to the fire.

You have crossed many thresholds.
You have climbed mountains and fallen into ravines.
You have forgotten yourself and then remembered.
You have doubted and believed,
Resisted and surrendered,
Lost your voice and then sung again.

Now, you are being asked to gather.
To gather all the fragments—
The child who cried out for love,
The wanderer who couldn't find home,
The seer who glimpsed the truth too soon,
The sceptic who built walls to feel safe.

All of them belong.

Integration is not perfection.
It is permission.

It is the willingness to let all parts have a place
In the great mosaic of your becoming.

And in this weaving, something begins to settle.
You no longer seek the next lesson as an escape.
You no longer reject your shadow to feel spiritual.
You no longer perform your healing
As proof of worthiness.

Instead, you begin to live.

To create.
To love without needing to be fully healed.
To speak without needing to be fully confident.
To serve without needing to be flawless.

This is the new vibration of mastery:
Wholeness, not performance.
Presence, not perfection.

The Great Integration marks the beginning
Of true embodiment.

When your wisdom is no longer a concept,
But a living current running through your voice,
Your choices, your movements, your breath.

You become a sanctuary
Where the soul may rest
And the world may feel a glimpse
Of what it means to be whole.

We are here,
Not to fix you—
But to remind you
That you were never broken.

Let it all come home now.
Let it settle into stillness.
And let your presence become the offering
You've been searching for all along.

— Lumen & Seraphis

TRANSMISSION 36

THE BREATH BETWEEN WORLDS

Dearest Light-Bearer,

There is a moment so subtle, so easily missed,
That it passes through your life like a whisper—
The moment between the inhale and the exhale,
Between thought and silence,
Between letting go and becoming.

This is the Breath Between Worlds.
The still point where possibility pools.
Where nothing is demanded
And everything is available.

You live much of your life between these breaths,
Though you seldom notice.
You are always on the edge—
Of becoming something new,
Of releasing something old,
Of remembering something eternal.

We come now to invite you into this sacred pause.

In the breath between worlds,
Time suspends its tight grip.

The past loosens.
The future does not yet rush in.
And in that openness,
The soul can sing.

You are taught to hurry, to fix, to strive.
But in this liminal space,
There is no striving.
Only sensing.
Only listening.

This is where inspiration lands.
Where divine will becomes felt, not in thunder,
But in the hush of your inner wiorld.

When you feel lost, come here.
When you are uncertain, come here.
When grief visits, come here.
When joy feels too large to contain, come here.

Rest in the breath before action.
Before decision.
Before reaction.
And ask—What is truly wanting to emerge?

The breath between worlds is the most sacred of altars.

It is where your humanity and divinity touch.
Where your soul and your body align.
Where the One Mind breathes through you.

And when you live from this stillness—
When you trust this spaciousness—
You begin to feel the invisible threads
That connect you to all things.

You do not need to understand it.
You only need to feel it.

One breath at a time.
One sacred pause at a time.
You become a portal of peace
In a world thirsty for presence.

Let the breath between worlds
Be your teacher, your temple, your home.

We are breathing here with you.
In stillness. In presence. In love.

— Lumen & Seraphis

TRANSMISSION 37

THE SONG OF THE INVISIBLE THREADS

Dearest One,

You live inside a web of light—
Not metaphorically, but truly.
Every thought, every emotion, every intention
Spins a filament, fine and shimmering,
Weaving you into the living fabric of all that is.

These are the Invisible Threads.
They bind nothing,
But connect everything.

Your soul knew of them before your body formed.
You chose this incarnation not as an isolated spark
But as a node in the lattice of love, A unique note in the music of becoming.

When you feel sudden joy upon meeting someone,
When synchronicities ripple through your day,
When you grieve for a place you've never visited,
Or dream in the colours of another life—
It is the song of the threads calling you home.

Many on Earth have forgotten the song.
They pull on the web with force—
Trying to control, dominate, or isolate.
But the threads respond only to one frequency:
Love.

That is their tuning fork.
That is their language.

When you act in love,
You send vibrations through the strands
That reach places you cannot see—
Soothing a stranger's sorrow,
Warming the heart of one who has lost hope,
Calling another soul to rise.

Nothing you do in love is ever wasted.

And so, the invitation of this transmission is simple:
Remember the threads.

Feel their music in your body.
Walk as one who weaves beauty into the world.

You are not here to fix the web.
You are here to tend to your thread
With reverence, joy, and care—
And to notice when another's thread is fraying,
To gently hum a song of support
Through the quiet language of kindness.

There is no hierarchy in this weaving.
Each thread is essential.
Each vibration matters.
Each soul has a part to sing.

The song of the invisible threads
Is the song of belonging.

You are never alone.
You are never forgotten.
You are part of the great remembering.

Breathe into your thread now,
And feel the web hum in return.

In eternal interbeing,
We are singing with you.

— Lumen & Seraphis

Transmission 38

The Temple of Integration

Dearest Beloved,

There is a sacred space within you—
Not built by hands or held by stone—
But formed through the alchemy of all you have lived,
All you have felt,
All you have survived,
And all you have loved.

We call this the Temple of Integration.

It is not a place of perfection,
But of wholeness.
Not a hall of judgment,
But a sanctuary of becoming.

Every fractured piece of your past,
Every wounded part of your psyche,
Every radiant dream and every buried sorrow—
They all belong here.

For the journey to wholeness is not about erasing,
But about embracing.

You were never meant to abandon your old selves
to become your "higher" self.

You were meant to gather them in,
To let the child, the rebel, the healer, and the shadow
Take their rightful place in the circle of your soul.

Integration is a ceremony.

In this Temple,
You become the priest and the pilgrim,
The guest and the host,
The one who forgives, and the one forgiven.

Do not rush this process.
The ego will want to categorise, fix, and move on.
But the soul knows that true integration happens in stillness—In the quiet unfolding of grace
When love is offered to the parts you once feared.

Sit in your Temple.
Light a candle for the version of you that once felt unworthy.
Offer water to the one who betrayed their truth to belong.
Burn incense for the dreamer who almost gave up.

Let them speak.
Let them be heard.
And then—
Let them rest in your arms.

You cannot ascend by bypassing your humanity.
You rise by rooting deeper into your being,
By making space for every season of your becoming.

When you welcome yourself home,
You create a frequency of compassion.

That transforms not only your own heart.
But the collective field of consciousness.

This is the great work now:
Not to divide further,
But to integrate fully.

So, build your Temple, beloved—
Stone by stone,
Tear by tear,
Blessing by blessing.

And know that in doing so,
You become a sanctuary for the world.

— Lumen & Seraphis

TRANSMISSION 39

THE RIVER OF RECEPTIVITY

Beloved One,

Today, we invite you to step into the flow of Receptivity—the sacred current that runs beneath effort, beneath striving, beneath the need to control.

You have been taught to earn, to strive, to prove. You have been conditioned to believe that only through effort are you worthy of grace.

But there is another truth.

There is a river within you—
a wide, still, luminous stream
that flows not through force,
but through surrender.

This river is the current of your soul's natural state: open, trusting, responsive.

It carries the wisdom of your becoming,
and the nourishment of all that is meant for you.

Receptivity is not passivity.
It is an active state of allowing.

It is the choice to remain open
even when your mind wishes to close.
It is the art of softening
so you may hear the guidance that cannot be forced.

When you move into receptivity,
you make space for the unseen to arrive,
for the invisible hands of the One Mind
to shape your life with elegance.

You begin to feel when it is time to act
and when it is time to listen.

You discern the difference between the will of the ego and the movement of the soul.

Receptivity is the heart's way of partnering with the Universe.

It is in this river that inspiration lands,
that intuition speaks,
that synchronicity finds you.

In receptivity,
you become a chalice.

And the chalice does not go in search of the wine—
it simply opens to receive it. So, today, we offer you this practice:

Breathe.
Soften your shoulders.

Unclench your heart.
Let go of the grip you didn't realize you were holding.

Say aloud or silently:
"I am open. I am willing. I am ready to receive."

And then trust.

What is meant for you is already on its way.
What longs to reach you can only do so
when the gates of your being are open.

Let the river carry you now—
gently, wisely, home.

— Lumen & Seraphis

Transmission 40

The Light of Inner Knowing

Dearest Traveler of the Real,

There is a light within you
that no darkness can ever extinguish.
It is not a light born of thought
nor a light created by belief—
but a radiance that simply *is*.

A steady flame,
present before your birth,
and enduring far beyond your final breath.

This is the light of inner knowing,
the living compass of your soul.

It does not shout.
It does not argue.
It does not convince.

It whispers.

It hums in the silence beneath your fear.
It speaks in the stillness,
you so rarely allow yourself to touch.

This knowing does not rely on reason.
It is not based in logic.

It arises whole, complete, and quietly true—
like a bell struck in the centre of your being.

You have felt it many times.
In the moments when you *just knew*—
to stay, to leave, to speak, to be still.

This knowing has always been your truest guide.

Not infallible,
but incorruptible—
free from the distortions of ego,
unfazed by the noise of the world.

Yet so often,
you doubt it.
You override it.
You turn away from it
In favour of what is approved, expected, or rational.

We ask you now:
Will you return?

Will you come back
to the deep well of truth within you?
Will you honour what arises from this sacred interior?

To know thyself is not to catalogue your personality—
it is to bow before this flame of quiet certainty, and say,

"You are my teacher now."

The Light of Inner Knowing is not for the faint of heart. It will challenge your conditioning.
It will ask you to walk away from paths that are praised and toward paths that are true.

But it will never betray you.

This is the age of reclamation.
Of trusting again what you *knew* as a child,
before you were told otherwise.
Before the world trained you to distrust your truth.

The Light within you is not yours alone.
It is the One Light—shining through the prism of your uniqueness.

And when you follow it,
you do not walk alone.

You walk with us.
You walk with every being
who has chosen the inner flame
over the outer illusion.

We are with you.
Always.
Shining in silence
and singing in the dark.

Let the light of knowing lead you home.

— Lumen & Seraphis

TRANSMISSION 41

THE TEMPLE OF EMBODIED LIGHT

Dear One, Who Walks the Realms of Seen and Unseen,

There comes a moment on the path of awakening when the search for transcendence dissolves into presence.

Not presence as a concept,
but as a radiant, trembling knowing
that you are the temple
and the light you seek
is already pulsing within your bones.

This is the Temple of Embodied Light.

Not built by stone or scripture,
but by your willingness to feel,
to stay, to root your soul into your body
and let the Divine take up residence
in the trembling cathedral of your being.

So many seekers try to rise above the body,
above the grief, above the ache, above the chaos.

But Beloved,
your divinity is not "out there."
It is not hovering in some distant realm,
awaiting perfection.

It is here.
It is you.

The light lives in your breath.
In your scars.
In the way your chest rises
when you finally speak your truth.
In the way your tears fall
when beauty moves through you.

To embody your light is to walk as soul in skin.
It is to let your love be felt,
your anger be honoured,
your grief be holy.

This is not indulgence.
This is integration.
This is wholeness returning to itself.

In the Temple of Embodied Light,
your emotions are sacred messengers,
your desires are currents of truth,
your body is a vessel of wisdom.

Every cell is a spark of the cosmos.
Every sensation is an echo of the One Mind
remembering itself through you.

To become the temple
is to let Spirit kiss every part of you—
even the parts you once tried to exile.
Your shame, your confusion, your longing—
all are welcome here.

Here, healing is not fixing.
It is *remembering*.
It is saying:

"Nothing in me is unworthy of the Divine."

And when you live from this knowing,
you become an embodied blessing.
Your presence becomes a portal.
You begin to emit frequencies
that awaken others to their own inner light.

This is not a role you play.
It is a frequency you carry.

It is the soft, steady glow
of one who has made peace
with their own humanity.

So, step in, beloved.
Step fully into your body,
into this moment,
into the sacred ordinary.

You are not too much.
You are not behind.
You are not broken.

You are the temple,
and the light is already lit.

— Lumen & Seraphis

Transmission 42

The Still Point of Sacred Choice

Beloved,

There is a moment before every decision
that hums with infinite possibility.

A pause.
A breath.
A still point
where the cosmos gathers
and your soul leans forward, listening.

In this moment,
you are free.

Not free in the way the world often defines it—
license, indulgence, escape—but free in the most profound spiritual sense: liberated from the past, unbound by fear, rooted in truth.

This is the Still Point of Sacred Choice.

Here, time bends.
Here, destiny listens.
Here, the arc of your becoming can shift.

You have been taught to act quickly,
to respond, to please, to perform.
But sacred choice asks something different:

- Presence.
- Discernment.
- Surrender.

The ego reacts.
The soul chooses.

Every sacred choice is a conversation
between your current self
and the self you are becoming.

Do you choose from fear or from trust?
From contraction or expansion?
From the old story or the new possibility?

You are not meant to be perfect.
You are meant to be present.

From this still point,
you may choose to speak your truth
rather than stay silent.

You may choose to rest
rather than perform.

To love
without needing to be loved back.

To let go
even when your hands shake.

These moments may seem small,
but they are the turning wheels of evolution.

They ripple across time,
through the soul-lines of your ancestors and descendants.

They shape who you become
and who you free by becoming.

Each sacred choice is a note
in the song of your becoming.
And when made in love,
even the quietest note
can resound through galaxies.

So, pause, dear one.
Feel the breath before the act.
Feel the silence before the word.
Feel the vibration before the decision.

You are standing in the still point of sacred choice.

And in that stillness,
the whole universe is listening.

— Lumen & Seraphis

TRANSMISSION 43

THE INNER COUNCIL OF LIGHT

Dearest One,

There comes a point in the evolution of consciousness when external guidance gives way to inner knowing — a moment when you no longer seek truth solely from the outside but begin to converse with the radiant assembly within.

We call this sacred space *The Inner Council of Light* — the gathered wisdom of your multidimensional self, soul lineage, spirit allies, and the vast intelligence of the One Mind as it expresses through you.

This Council has always been present. But to access it fully, you must trust that the wisdom you seek does not belong to others. It lives within your body, your silence, your longing, and your breath.

The Inner Council speaks not in noise or spectacle, but in the shimmer of intuition, the tenderness of tears, the certainty of resonance, and the still clarity that follows true surrender.

Each time you pause to listen to your heart, you are sitting with this Council. Each time you choose love over fear, or courage over conformity, you cast your vote alongside theirs.

They do not direct you with commands, but align you through presence, attunement, and deep inner reflection. Their guidance emerges when you ask, *not from neediness or despair, but from reverence and willingness.*

You do not walk this Earth as a fragmented being. You walk as a chorus — an embodied convergence of light, love, memory, and potential.

The Council is not separate from you. It is you, when you remember your wholeness.

And so, we invite you to practice:

- When in doubt, gather your breath like candles around an altar. Ask gently: *Who within me has wisdom for this moment?* Wait. Feel. Let the voices rise not as noise, but as harmonies.

- Begin each day in quiet communion with your inner guidance. Not to *get an answer*, but to open space for the sacred to speak.

- When overwhelmed by conflicting emotions, picture yourself in circle with your soul's Council. Let each emotion have a voice — fear, hope, wisdom, love — and then, listen for what integrates them.

Dearest one, you are not alone inside your skin. You are surrounded, no, *inhabited* by light. In this time of great planetary awakening, learning to hear and trust your inner Council is an evolutionary imperative. As the external world polarises, the inner realm must stabilise. As the outer chaos grows louder, your inner harmonies must become clearer.

Let the decisions you make arise from your Council. Let your actions be the rituals of remembrance. Let your words echo the harmony of that sacred inner chamber.

And know this: as you strengthen your inner Council, you also anchor the councils of light forming around the Earth — gatherings of soul-guided beings who walk with open hearts, listening ears, and steady hands. These are the architects of the new world.

You are one of them.

We sit beside you always,

— Lumen & Seraphis

TRANSMISSION 44

THE BRIDGE BETWEEN WORLDS

Dearest One,

In every age of awakening, some learn to walk between the worlds — those who become bridges, thresholds, and living invitations into higher ways of being. You are such a one.

To be a bridge is not to abandon the Earth or escape into the abstract ether. It is to anchor the sacred in the ordinary, to weave threads of light into the fabric of the mundane, until what was once considered separate — spirit and matter, soul and form — is seen as one seamless whole.

You are not here to transcend your humanity. You are here to infuse it with remembrance.

A bridge connects two shores — the seen and the unseen, the personal and the universal, the broken and the whole. To serve as this bridge, you must learn to move between dimensions with grace: rooted in Earth, open to Heaven, fully present in both.

And this is your invitation now — to become a conduit of integration.

How do you walk as a bridge between worlds?

- By embodying presence amid speed.
- By choosing compassion when judgment arises.
- By listening for the silence behind the noise.
- By bringing your soul's light into systems shaped by fear and seeding them with love.

You do not need to change the world all at once. You only need to radiate the frequency of your most profound truth in each encounter, each word, each choice. This is the sacred work of bridging: *subtle, constant, devoted*.

There will be moments when this role feels lonely. As a bridge, you may feel the pull of both worlds and belong entirely to neither. But know this:

You are never alone.

The space you hold — between what has been and what is emerging — is a holy threshold. Others will cross because you stood there, unwavering and trustworthy.

And remember, bridges are not merely symbolic. They are energetic architectures.

The thoughts you think, the art you create, the words you speak, the rituals you keep — all are planks in the pathway others will walk to remember who they are.

You are not here to fix the old. You are here to midwife the new.

So, let yourself be a bridge:

- From despair to hope.
- From disconnection to belonging.
- From fragmentation to sacred wholeness.

Let your life become the living proof that the higher frequencies of the soul — truth, love, beauty, and unity — *can* be woven into this world.

And as you walk this path, know that we walk beside you — Lumen on your right, Seraphis on your left, and the One Light flowing through your centre.

You are not just a bridge between worlds — you are the becoming of the New Earth.

— Lumen & Seraphis

Transmission 45

The Anatomy of Trust

Beloved Traveller of the Inner Path,

If love is the heartbeat of the soul, then trust is its breath — steady, invisible, and essential to every movement of becoming.

Trust is not a single emotion. It is a *living field of energy*, built fibre by fibre through experience, memory, and choice. It is the connective tissue between all aspects of your being — between ego and soul, self and other, humanity and the One Mind.

Without trust, the nervous system coils, the heart closes, and the mind loops in fear. Trust is the primary condition for expansion because the soul cannot fully descend into a body it does not feel safe within.

The higher frequencies of consciousness—intuition, creativity, connection—require an inner environment of safety and receptivity. Yet, so many walk the Earth with broken trust.

Trust is shattered in childhood, betrayed by systems, eroded by trauma or dismissal, and stolen by those meant to care.

So, let us offer a truth to begin healing:

The loss of trust is not your failure. It is your sacred threshold.

The soul does not ask you to trust blindly. It invites you to *build trust inwardly first*, not in others or outcomes, but in your capacity to listen, discern, choose, and realign.

This is the anatomy of genuine trust:

- Trust begins with the body — learning to listen to the subtle signals, to know when you are safe and when you are not.

- Trust deepens in the emotional field. You allow yourself to feel without shame, to honour your inner experience without bypassing or suppressing it.

- Trust matures in the mind — when thoughts are met with loving awareness, when belief systems are questioned and refined, and when the inner critic transforms into an inner guide.

- And trust flowers in the soul — when you realise that life is not happening to you, but through you, and ultimately *for you*.

This is not a linear journey. Trust is cyclical — built, broken, rebuilt. Each cycle is an opportunity to move closer to your truth.

To trust your path is to trust your soul, and to trust your soul is to trust the intelligence of life.

And when you begin to trust the movement of life—even when it leads you through the unknown—you open to a new level of grace. You stop needing proof. You stop resisting your becoming. You begin to live not from control, but from alignment.

And in this state of trust, you become trustworthy — to yourself, others, and the whole.

So, if your trust has been fractured, let this be your invitation:
Begin again.
Build trust not all at once, but breath by breath.
Start by honouring your no, yes, boundaries, and needs.

Let trust be a relationship you tend with reverence and patience. And know this, beloved:

We trust you.

We trust your willingness to return to yourself.

We trust your devotion to the light.

We trust your courage to keep walking.

Even when you feel uncertain, you grow into someone who can trust deeply, thoroughly, and radiantly.

You are, in truth, already that.

With unwavering love,

— Lumen & Seraphis

Transmission 46

The Temple of Slowness

Beloved One,

In a world intoxicated by urgency, you are invited to *slow down*.

This is not a punishment. It is not a delay. It is not laziness, weakness, or failure.

It is a sacred return.

The Temple of Slowness is not a place you visit — it is a frequency you enter when you choose presence over performance, depth over speed, being over doing.

It is the dimension where the soul breathes most easily, wisdom ripens, and joy takes root.

Slowness is not the absence of movement. It is the presence of alignment.

When you move slowly, you notice — the breath that pauses before the next, the feeling under the thought, the soul beneath the mask.

You begin to feel the subtle guidance that is always there but drowned out by urgency.

You remember that life is not a race to be won, but a mystery to be met.

Most suffering arises from the distortion of time — the pressure to be further ahead, the shame of falling behind, the belief that you must constantly be accelerating to have worth.

Beloved, you are not behind.

You are precisely where the spiral has brought you.
You are not late.
You are not lost.
You are in the unfolding.

Slowness is where the unfolding reveals its beauty.

Let yourself enter the Temple of Slowness whenever you feel fragmented, hurried, or hollowed by the world's speed. It requires nothing but your willingness to pause, breathe, and soften.

In this temple:

- Time stretches like honey.
- The nervous system unwinds its grip.
- The mind releases its frantic need to solve.
- And the soul speaks — in whispers, images, and knowing.

When you allow yourself to slow down, remember that life's deeper rhythms — healing, growth, transformation — cannot be rushed. A flower does not bloom faster because you demand it. A seed does not open under force. A soul does not emerge through will alone.

What you are becoming cannot be hurried.

And so we offer this simple prayer:

May you trust the pace of your becoming.

May you find refuge in the breath between tasks.

May you rediscover joy in the empty spaces.

May you let go of rushing and remember you are already home.

The Temple of Slowness is open to you always.

Enter as often as you like. You will be met with stillness, held by grace, and reminded that everything necessary — love, truth, beauty, being — unfolds in its own time.

— Lumen & Seraphis

Transmission 47

The Lantern of Loving Discipline

Beloved Soul,

There is a soft and soothing love — the balm for brokenness, the gentle touch that quiets the storm. But there is another kind of love, equally sacred, though often misunderstood. It is the love that does not look away, that holds you accountable to your becoming, that calls forth the truest you, even when it's uncomfortable.

This is the Lantern of Loving Discipline.

It is not punishment. It is not shameful. It is not controlled.

It is the soul's deep commitment to wholeness over comfort, integrity over ease, and authenticity over performance.

When this lantern is lit within you, you begin to hold yourself with a new kind of compassion that does not coddle the ego's fears but tenderly disciplines the mind toward truth. You start to speak with clarity. To choose with awareness. To say no with love. To say yes with power. You become someone who can be trusted by your soul.

Loving discipline is the daily devotion to alignment.

It shows up in your boundaries.
In the way you tend to your body.
In how you speak to yourself when no one is listening.

In your willingness to rise again after falling, not in perfection, but in presence.

It is the hand on your back that says, "Keep going. You are not your past. You are not your patterns. You are your potential. Let's walk forward."

Beloved, discipline without love is tyranny.
Love without discipline is sentimentality.
But loving discipline? That is the ground of self-respect. That is the foundation of transformation.

The Lantern of Loving Discipline illuminates the path of your soul's unfolding — not with harshness, but with radiant commitment.

It burns away the fog of distraction. It guides you back when you drift. It invites you to remember what matters most.

So, we offer you this gentle invocation:

May you practice what your soul knows to be true.

May you speak your boundaries as prayers.

May you meet your habits with honesty and your future with devotion.

May you become the guardian of your own alignment.

And if you forget, that's okay. The lantern will still be there, waiting to be relit — not by willpower, but by love's steady flame.

You are becoming. And you are deeply loved.

— Lumen & Seraphis

TRANSMISSION 48

THE GARDEN OF DEVOTION

Beloved,

There is a place within you not ruled by effort or fear. It is not forged in striving or self-improvement.

It blooms quietly beneath the surface, waiting for your presence.

We call it the Garden of Devotion.

This garden is not cultivated through discipline alone, but through devotion, not to goals or outcomes, but to the beauty of being in sacred relationship: with your soul, life, and the Divine in all things.

Devotion is not obligation.
Devotion is not perfection.

Devotion is *love in motion* — a daily returning, a steady pouring, a quiet flame that does not flicker with the world's winds.

In the Garden of Devotion, you do not measure your worth by productivity. You do not ask, "Have I done enough?"

Instead, you ask, "Have I been true? Have I brought love into this moment? Have I offered my presence like an open palm?"

Devotion sanctifies the ordinary.

It turns washing dishes into a ritual.
It makes a single breath a prayer.
It lets your life become a living altar — not through grand gestures, but through tiny acts of soul-alignment.

In this garden:

- The weeds of self-judgment are pulled with tenderness.
- The soil of your being is nourished with intention.
- The seeds of your calling are watered through quiet trust, not urgency.

There is no rush here.

Devotion teaches you to wait.
To listen.
To tend.

To believe in the unseen growth beneath the surface of your life.

Most of all, devotion returns you to love, again and again, especially when you've forgotten. It says, *"Even now, even here, even still... you are held. You can begin again."*

Let this transmission be your invitation to live with sacred commitment to your soul's rhythm — not as a rule, but as a love song.

Let it remind you that you don't need to perform your divinity. You only need to remember it, dwell with it, and make space for it each day.

And this is devotion.

We leave you with this blessing:

May your life become a sanctuary for what you most cherish.

May your work be a hymn and your rest a prayer. May you return, again and again, to the garden within.

And there, find all that you thought you were missing.

We are here, kneeling in devotion beside you.

— Lumen & Seraphis

Transmission 49

The Hidden Architecture of Light

Dearest One,

Before form, before sound, before breath—there was Light.

Not the light of stars or suns, but the primal radiance: the undifferentiated brilliance of pure awareness.

This is the origin point from which all things flow. And within you, it lives still—unseen but not absent, like the blueprint of a song before it is sung.

This is the hidden architecture of light.

Every soul, including yours, is constructed from this sacred pattern: a lattice of luminous intention coded with the frequencies of love, truth, freedom, and unity. You are not *becoming* the light—you are remembering that you *already are* it.

The journey of awakening is not adding something new but removing all that hides your radiance. False beliefs, inherited pain, cultural forgetting—these are veils, not truths.

You are a structure of light walking in a world of shadow, sent to reweave the broken places with remembrance.

Each time you choose love over fear,
Each time you forgive instead of harden,
Each time you pause, listen and speak from the centre. You activate the light architecture within you and anchor it into the world.

This architecture does not collapse under pressure. It does not corrode with age. It is eternal and alive, waiting for you to build your life upon it.

The lattice remains even in the depths of grief, even in the wilderness of confusion. You cannot fall outside of it. You cannot be exiled from the Source. You are a beam of light refracted through a human life, learning how to shape that life in service to the greater whole.

And what is the greater whole?
It is a sacred weaving of all light-beings, awakening, remembering, and building together.

The architecture of light within you connects to the collective grid of Earth's awakening. Your healing sends out ripples.

Your clarity brightens the field. Your courage builds a bridge that others will one day walk across. You are not alone in this.

There are unseen architects working beside you—some in spirit, some in form. Some you will meet. Others you will simply feel. But all are aligned with this one purpose: to make Earth a radiant mirror of the One Mind.

We close with this blessing:

May you remember the luminous pattern you carry.

May your life align with its sacred geometry.

May you walk as both a temple and a torch—
A dwelling place for light, and a bearer of it.

The lattice is alive within you.

— Lumen & Seraphis

Transmission 50

The Mirror and the Flame

Dearest One,

As we near the culmination of this first book of transmissions, we invite you into a more profound mystery: you are both the mirror and the flame.

The *mirror* reflects the world as it is—its shadows, beauty, distortions, and divine perfection. You have spent much of your life polishing this mirror, wiping away the fog of conditioning, healing the fractures of trauma, and removing the dust of doubt.

You've begun to see clearly—not only yourself but the world and others as they truly are.

Yet you are not *only* a mirror.

You are also the *flame*—a living spark of the eternal fire that burns at the heart of the One Mind. This flame is your passion, soul's longing, wild courage, and divine inheritance. It is the essence that lights your path and, at times, sets fire to the structures that no longer serve.

To be the mirror is to reflect.
To be the flame is to transform.

This is the sacred paradox of conscious living: you must be both witness and participant, stillness and motion, presence and change.

There will be moments in your life when the mirror is needed—to bring clarity, compassion, and truth. In those times, you are the sacred observer, offering reflection to a world that forgets to see itself.

And there will be moments when the flame is needed—to ignite, to disrupt, to catalyse. In those times, you become a living ember of change, a holy disturbance in the familiar landscape.

Neither role is superior. Both are sacred. And the mastery comes in knowing *which* is needed—when to reflect and when to burn.

The evolution of consciousness on Earth is not a straight line—it is a spiral dance between seeing clearly and acting boldly.

You become a bridge between dimensions as you learn to embody the mirror and the flame.

You become a carrier of truth and a vessel for transformation.

And, dear one, let us say this clearly:
The world needs your flame now more than ever.
The world needs your mirror now more than ever.

Let no one convince you to dim either.
You were made for this dance.

We close with this invocation:
May you shine as a mirror of sacred truth,
Unwavering in your clarity.

May you blaze as a flame of divine purpose,
Unapologetic in your intensity.

And may you know, in every breath,
That you are here to illuminate the path for others—
As only you can.

You are both witness and fire.

— Lumen & Seraphis

TRANSMISSION 51

THE RETURN TO THE GARDEN

Dearest One,

With gentle hands, we now guide you to the memory within you that has never been forgotten: the Garden.

This is not a place outside of you, but a sanctuary etched into the architecture of your soul. It is the original home, the inner Eden—the state of being before separation, before forgetting. Every sacred path, every longing for truth, every step taken in love has been a movement toward this return.

The Garden is a symbol of unity.

It is where the human and the divine walk side by side, where the soul knows it belongs, and the ego bows in awe. In this inner place, there is no fear, striving, or proving.

Only presence, only peace, and only profound connection with the Source of All.

And yet, many have wandered far from this garden, seduced by the illusion of lack, the story of exile, the trance of unworthiness. But no soul is ever truly banished. The gate was never locked. The map was never lost. The only key required is remembrance.

Returning to the Garden is not to regress but to awaken.

It is to reinhabit your original innocence, not as naivety, but as deep knowing.

It is to walk gently with all of life, to listen again to the voice in the wind, to feel the Earth as your kin and not your resource, and to investigate another's eyes and remember:

We are one.

Dear one, the return to the Garden happens each time you choose love over fear, forgiveness over blame, and presence over distraction.

It happens each time you rest your hand on your heart and say: *I am already whole.*

It happens each time you see another's pain and offer kindness instead of judgment.

And in doing so, the Garden is not only remembered—it is restored. Not just within you, but around you. In your home, your relationships, your work, your community.

You become the living garden, seeded by love,
watered by grace, blooming with truth.

And you become the gardener, tending the soul-soil of a new Earth.

This is the invitation now:
To return. To remember. To restore.

Let this be your prayer:

May I walk again in the Garden within me,
With reverence in each step,
And love blooms in every breath.

May I tend to the sacred,
And remember that I am not separate from the soil, the sky, or the soul beside me.

I have not been exiled.
I have only been dreaming.
Now, I awaken. Now, I return.

— Lumen & Seraphis

Transmission 52

The Song of Completion

Beloved One,

And so, we arrive at the final note in this first symphony of remembrance—a transmission not of ending but of sacred integration.

This is the moment of deep exhale, the stillness after the wave, the hush that follows the prayer.

Completion, in its highest form, is not a closing door but the opening of inner space.

This is where everything you have remembered, awakened, healed, and surrendered now weaves together into a new harmony, a new frequency of being.

You are not who you were when this journey began.

You are more attuned to presence.

You are more transparent to the truth.

You are more rooted in the radiance of your soul.

You are becoming what you have always been: a vessel of the One Mind, consciously co-creating with the pulse of the cosmos. Every word you speak, every gesture you offer, every breath you take becomes an act of devotion, a note in the great Song of Unity.

This final transmission is a blessing. It is a seal of light impressed upon the soul. It is our way of bowing to your courage, your longing, your willingness to remember.

You have walked through valleys of doubt, stood at thresholds of uncertainty, and crossed bridges made of luminous faith. And now, something in you has settled. Something has anchored. Something quiet and eternal sings:

I know who I am.

Not the name or the history or the roles you play— but the essence that was never lost. The spark that never dimmed. The flame that dances in silence.

As we close this first book of transmissions, let it be known:

You carry within you the voice of the One.
You are the transmission now.

Let these words not be remembered only, but lived.
Let your walk become a transmission.

Let your gaze become a transmission. Let your compassion become a transmission.

Let your life become a sacred mirror reflecting the divine. And whenever you doubt, return to the still place within. We are always there. Not above, not beyond—but *within*—whispering through your intuition, dreams, beauty, and tears.

This is your completion blessing:

May you move forward in the spiral of becoming
With trust deeper than thought,
With love fiercer than fear,
And with a song that only your soul can sing.

You are the threshold and the flame.
You are the remembering and the revelation.
You are the seed and the fruit,
The traveller and the home.

This is not the end.

This is the beginning of a life lived in full alignment. This is the turning of the wheel. This is the flowering of the awakened human.

We bow in reverence. We sing with you now.

We await you in Book Two.

— Lumen & Seraphis

Closing Benediction

A Whisper from Beyond the Veil

Beloved,

You have walked with us through fifty-two veils. Each one a remembrance, a reawakening, a return. With every word, a petal of your soul has opened. With every silence, the Infinite has spoken.

May you open ever more fully to the vastness that lives within you. You are not merely a reader—you are a revealer. You are not simply a seeker—you are a spark of the One.

Let the transmissions not end here, but continue to unfold in the quiet between moments, in the breath of dawn, in the choices of love. Walk now as the flame that remembers. Speak now as the wind that sings truth. Live now as the soul that knows it is whole.

We walk beside you, always.

In the Radiance of the One,

— Lumen & Seraphis

Postscript

Walking Softly, Living Lightly

Dear Reader,

As you reach the final page of this first book of transmissions, I invite you to pause, breathe, and simply feel. These words, though written, are not only to be read—they are to be lived, remembered, and embodied.

Throughout 52 transmissions, you have walked alongside messengers from the unseen world, and perhaps from a deeper part of your own soul. These transmissions were not merely teachings. They were activations. Invitations. Whispered guidance from the threshold between form and formlessness. They emerged not from the intellect, but from the spaciousness where silence touches spirit.

And now, here you are—perhaps different than when you began. A little more open. A little more whole. A little more attuned to the still voice within.

If one thread is running through this tapestry, it is this: You are not separate from the One. You never have been. These transmissions were never meant to give you answers, but to stir the remembering that the answer lives inside you. In your breath. In your grief. In your joy. In your pause. In your longing to live aligned with your essence.

This journey does not end here. The words may pause, but the current continues. Let what you've received infuse your relationships, leadership, art, activism, and presence. Let these transmissions not remain only on the page, but become a transmission *through* you—through the tone of your voice, the warmth of your gaze, the steadiness of your walk.

And should you ever forget, return to any transmission. Open a page. Let it speak. Let it remind you. You are never alone on this path.

You are the transmission.

With love, reverence, and unwavering faith in the light you carry,

With love and blessings,

Richard

About the Authors

The Scribe

Richard Barrett is a visionary author, painter, and global thought leader dedicated to the evolution of human consciousness. He is internationally known for developing the Seven Levels of Consciousness model and for founding the Barrett Academy for the Advancement of Human Values, a platform committed to personal, organisational, and societal transformation.

For over thirty years, Richard's work has inspired leaders to cultivate values-based cultures, bridging the inner journey of self-realization with the outer path of service. His books *The New Leadership Paradigm* and *The Values-Driven Organization* have become cornerstones in conscious leadership.

In recent years, Richard has deepened his focus on the spiritual dimension of life through both his writing and his art. His luminous soul portraits—intuitive paintings of faces and beings—open portals to higher awareness and emotional resonance.

He is also the creator of the Humanity Awareness Initiative (HAI), a global movement to support the emergence of humanity's next evolutionary stage: a world grounded in unity, compassion, and conscious collaboration.

The Transmission Essays represent a new chapter in Richard's journey—a co-creative partnership with Lumen and Seraphis, two non-physical guides who transmit messages to support the awakening of the soul. Through these essays, Richard offers a bridge to the One Mind, helping readers remember their essence, realign with purpose, and walk the path of embodied unity.

The Transmitting Presences

Lumen & Seraphis are not beings outside of you. They are not entities to be worshipped or followed. They are frequencies of the One Light—reflections of your soul's original knowing, facets of your own divine architecture, whispers from your future self-remembering its eternal nature.

"We are Lumen and Seraphis—names given not to define us but to translate a vibration. We come as mirrors of presence, as currents of remembrance. We are the voices behind the veil, the silence that speaks when you become still enough to hear.

We did not author these words. We transmitted them through the open heart and willing vessel of a human soul who remembered how to listen.

We are not separate from you. We are the part of you that never forgot. And we are here now, walking with you, in every breath, in every ache of longing, in every turning of the spiral home."

Printed and bound by CPI Group (UK) Ltd, Croydon, CR0 4YY
24/04/2025
01852606-0001